CAMBRIDGE LIBRARY COLLECTION

Books of enduring scholarly value

Women's Writing

The later twentieth century saw a huge wave of academic interest in women's writing, which led to the rediscovery of neglected works from a wide range of genres, periods and languages. Many books that were immensely popular and influential in their own day are now studied again, both for their own sake and for what they reveal about the social, political and cultural conditions of their time. A pioneering resource in this area is Orlando: Women's Writing in the British Isles from the Beginnings to the Present (http://orlando.cambridge.org), which provides entries on authors' lives and writing careers, contextual material, timelines, sets of internal links, and bibliographies. Its editors have made a major contribution to the selection of the works reissued in this series within the Cambridge Library Collection, which focuses on non-fiction publications by women on a wide range of subjects from astronomy to biography, music to political economy, and education to prison reform.

The Duties of Women

Frances Power Cobbe (1822–1904) was an Irish writer, social reformer and activist best known for her contributions to Victorian feminism. After the death of her father in 1857, Cobbe travelled extensively across Europe before becoming a leader-writer for the London newspaper *The Echo* in 1868. She continued to publish on the topics of feminism, social problems and theology for the rest of her life. This volume, first published in 1881, contains a series of essays discussing the ethical practice of feminism. Written during a transitional period for the movement, when calls for universal suffrage were becoming the defining feature of feminism, Cobbe advocates the need for women to practice a form of emancipation which does not conform to stereotypical views, in order to avoid a public backlash against universal suffrage. Emphasising the political importance of private behaviours, this volume demonstrates feminist responses to changes in nineteenth century feminism. For more information on this author, see http://orlando.cambridge.org/public/svPeople?person_id=cobbfr

T0382122

The Duties of Women

A Course of Lectures

FRANCES POWER COBBE

CAMBRIDGE
UNIVERSITY PRESS

CAMBRIDGE UNIVERSITY PRESS

Cambridge, New York, Melbourne, Madrid, Cape Town, Singapore,
São Paolo, Delhi, Dubai, Tokyo, Mexico City

Published in the United States of America by Cambridge University Press, New York

www.cambridge.org
Information on this title: www.cambridge.org/9781108021036

© in this compilation Cambridge University Press 2010

This edition first published 1881
This digitally printed version 2010

ISBN 978-1-108-02103-6 Paperback

THE

DUTIES OF WOMEN.

A COURSE OF LECTURES

BY

FRANCES POWER COBBE.

" Whatever any one does or says, I must be good ; just as if the
emerald were always saying this ; Whatever any one does or says, I
must be emerald and keep my colour."— *Marcus Aurelius*, vii. 15.

WILLIAMS AND NORGATE,

14, HENRIETTA STREET, COVENT GARDEN, LONDON, AND
20, SOUTH FREDERICK STREET, EDINBURGH.

1881.

LONDON :
G. NORMAN AND SON, PRINTERS, 29, MAIDEN LANE,
COVENT GARDEN.

CONTENTS.

PREFACE.

THE following Lectures, somewhat differently
arranged, were delivered last winter in London to an
audience of ladies, and were repeated at Clifton in the
ensuing spring. The reader will kindly bear in mind
that they were prepared with a view to such *viva voce*
use, and not for perusal in a book; and also that the
plan of their delivery included many extempore
illustrations and lighter remarks. A few of these only
have been preserved in the foot-notes of the present
volume.

My purpose in delivering these Lectures originally,
and now in publishing them, will become sufficiently
apparent as the reader proceeds; but to avoid the
risk of any possible misconstruction, I shall offer
here a short explanation of my *locus standi* as regards
the whole subject in question. I have been for many
years deeply interested in what is called the " Woman's
Movement," and have taken part in pleading for the

Higher Education of women; for the admission of women to University Degrees; for the protection of the property of Married women; for the Employment of women; for the protection of women from Aggravated Assaults; for the entrance of women into the Medical Profession; and, lastly, for extension of the Parliamentary Suffrage to women possessed of the requisite property qualification. Of the wisdom of many of these demands (so far as they were then formulated) I was not in my earlier life convinced. I was then of opinion that the happy duties of a daughter and mistress of a household which fell to my lot, together with village charities and literary and other pursuits, sufficiently filled up the life of a woman, without adding to them wider social and political aims. It was only after I had laboured for some time with my honoured friend Mary Carpenter, at Bristol, and learned to feel intense interest in the legislation which might possibly mitigate the evils of crime and pauperism, that I seriously asked myself (under the upbraiding of that good old Abolitionist S. J. May), *why* I should not seek for political representation as the direct and natural means of aiding every reform I had at heart? The answer was not long doubtful; and now for nearly a quarter of a century I have, as I have just said, associated myself to the best of my ability more or less with nearly all the movements

in England for the advancement of women. Looking
back over those years I find I have not lost one jot of
faith in the righteousness or expediency of our demands.
On the contrary, I have seen every year more reason to
regard the part hereafter to be played by women in
public affairs, as offering the best hope for the moral,
and still more emphatically, for the spiritual, interests
of humanity. I think more highly of women since I have
watched them with the calm eyes of middle age; and
I have more confidence than I had at first, both in their
ability and in their stability.

But it would be idle to veil from myself that the path
of progress on which women have now entered, and
which we have done our best to open for them, is a
road which leads up a steep Hill of Difficulty, and from
which there are turnings to the right and the left,
running down into all manner of quagmires and preci-
pices. So many indeed, and so grave are the dangers on
either hand, that I cannot blame those who see more to
fear than to hope from the movement in question,
and raise around us rather a cry of alarm than a cheer
of encouragement. But dangers must be faced whenever any time-honoured evil is to be swept away, or
any new good achieved. The woman's movement could
not now be stopped if we desired it, nor do we desire
to stop it if it lay at our option so to do. What we
wish to accomplish, and what it is our imperative duty to

strive to accomplish with all our might, is to direct aright the great progress in question; to set up sign posts of warning against those wrong turnings in the road which can only lead to destruction; and to point all eyes which we are permitted to direct, up to the straight, clear way before us—the one only safe, true way of progress,—the way of DUTY.

In brief, then, in addressing my countrywomen in this way, I have aimed at inciting them, in the first place, to give deep and well ordered reflection to the subject of morals in general, and of their own duties in particular; trusting that I might help them to see the fallacy of several errors which have hitherto misled us, and to recognize how noble and brave and beautiful is the ideal of womanly virtue to which we are bound to lift ourselves up. And, in the second place, I have striven to warn my hearers against that neglect of social *bienséances*, that adoption of looser and more "Bohemian" manners, and, worst of all, that fatal laxity of judgment regarding grave moral transgressions, which have appeared of late years amongst us as the inevitable extravagance of reaction from earlier strictness. These faults and mistakes constitute, I conceive, deadly perils to the whole movement for the advancement of women, and with all my strength I would implore every woman who sympathizes with that movement to set her face like a flint against them. It is our task to make Society *more* pure, *more* free from vice, either masculine or feminine, than it has ever been before, not to allow its law to become one shadow of a shade less rigid.

Men, especially Englishmen and Americans, are, as a rule, wonderfully generous to women. Thousands of them labour for their mothers, their wives, or their daughters all their lives long ; and the higher-minded are full of chivalrous indulgence for all women. If we count over with speechless indignation the hundreds of men who in our country yearly beat and trample their wretched wives to death, we must never allow that hideous fact—or any other of the many wrongs of our sex — to blind us to the counterbalancing truth that the average Englishman means well to women, and will make no small sacrifices for them ; and that there exist at least as many noble and high-hearted men, genuine champions of our sex, in Parliament and out of it, as there are wife-beating ruffians in the slums of Liverpool and London.

But with all their kindly feelings, their good intentions, their readiness to labour and sacrifice themselves for women, men give us most rarely that which we really want, not favour, but—*Justice.* Nothing is easier than to coax them to pet us like children ; nothing more difficult than to persuade them to treat us like responsible human beings. Only a small

number of them, it would seem, can yet be brought to
realize that we have not only mouths to be fed and
hearts to be comforted by faithful affection, but also
brains to be cultivated, and wills seeking also, like their
own, for the free use of whatever powers we may
inherit.   That a woman should really possess *Public
Spirit*, and that its exercise should be as ennobling to
her as it is to a man, this is a lesson which it takes
most men half a life time to learn.

It is not, then, from men, with all their kindness,
that we must look primarily for aid to climb the
ascent before us.   Even if they were more ready than
they now are to help us, they could do very little
beyond encouraging us by their sympathy and smooth-
ing a few obstacles out of our way.   Ours is the old,
old story of every uprising race, or class, or order.
The work of elevation must be wrought by ourselves
or not at all.   At this hour there are, I believe, in
England hundreds of women of the highest social and
intellectual rank who desire to see better days for
their sex, but who are sitting, waiting patiently for
some masculine Jupiter to descend and lift our chariot
out of the ruts of custom.   It is in vain !   They may
so wait for ever.   Even if Jupiter were to come down,.
women themselves would drive the car into another
rut the next moment.   Nothing but our own steady
and simultaneous labour can really elevate our sex.

Every woman who works wisely and well for any
good public cause (whether that cause directly concern
female interests or not), does her share in thus lifting
up the womanhood of the nation. And perhaps that
other woman does even more for the same end, whose
whole time is rightly absorbed in the perfect performance of her duties as daughter, wife, or mother,—but
who, from her place of honour, simply avows on all
fitting occasions, that she too shares indignation for
the wrongs, and sympathy with the aspirations of her
sisters.

Finally, I will only add that, greatly as I desire to
see the enfranchizement and elevation of women, I
consider even that object subordinate to the moral
character of each individual woman. If women were
to become less *dutiful* by being enfranchized,—less
conscientious, less unselfish, less temperate, less chaste,
—then I should say " For Heaven's sake, let us stay
where we are ! *Nothing* we can ever gain would be
worth such a loss." But I have yet to learn that
Freedom, which is the spring of all the nobler virtues in
Man, will be less the ground of loftier and purer
virtues in Woman. Nay, it is in firm faith that
women will be *more* dutiful than they have even been,
more conscientious, more unselfish, more temperate,
and more chaste, that I have joined my voice to
the demand for their emancipation, believing also that

in a wider sphere they will forget many a fault and
folly of the past, and will learn yet other virtues
which now they lack or have not enough learned to
exercise, — Courage and Truthfulness, Justice and
Public Spirit.

LECTURE I.

Introductory.

THE spectacle of the waste of precious things is always one of the saddest in this mysterious world. We are often called on to regret huge ships sunk in the sea, famous old books burnt or lost, beautiful temples shattered by shot and shell, harvests destroyed by storm or drought, and men with splendid gifts going down to an untimely grave, all their training for a life of usefulness ending in silence and oblivion.

But what are all these forms of waste compared to that which has been going on, in all lands and ages, of the lives of women—waste as regards the purposes either of their own moral growth or natural happiness, and waste of their faculties to make the world happier and better? Think of women's natures as meanly as we may, rank the powers wherewith they are endowed at the lowest possible estimation, still it is deplorable to reflect on the spendthrift reckless-ness wherewith they have been thrown away for no advantage to any living being, but merely for some

1

senseless prejudice. Iphigenia, sacrificed to make the
wind blow, was in truth a typical victim of supersti-
tious custom and masculine selfishness. A lark born to
sing its joyous little song at leisure far aloft in the blue
sky, caught and shut up in a cage in a sordid city lane,
scarcely suffers a more grievous wrong than the souls
of myriads of our sisters cooped in gynecæums and
zenanas, and harems and convents, and in many a
home little better than a nunnery or a seraglio.*

There is in all young girls a touching capacity for finding innocent enjoyment in the smallest and simplest
things, a capacity which, as we look back on it in
later years, fills our old hearts with yearning and regret.
But while the similar pleasures of boys are usually
amply studied and provided for even at their schools,
it is not very often, except in the happiest families
and among the wisest parents and teachers, that little
girls are encouraged or permitted to take their fill of

---

* A gentleman, long a missionary in India, has told me that
it is not at all an uncommon case for a Hindoo woman of the
upper ranks to be carried to her grave, never having put her foot
to the ground in the open air in her life. Her entire existence
has been spent among the wretched puerilities and sensualities
of the zenana. Yet these are the women who, when they have
a chance, display (as Mr. Mill witnessed) exceptional powers of
statesmanship; and several of whom are now distinguishing
themselves as poetesses and novelists. The condition of a
woman with such latent faculties cramped into the zenana
life under a tyrannical husband or mother-in-law must be
miserable beyond conception. Her soul must ache like a
Chinese woman's foot in her shoe.

the delights of air and exercise, while their limbs yet
crave, by Nature's beneficent law, for free and incessant
motion, and their young hearts can drink in the joys of
the sunshine and the flowers in all their May-morning
freshness. Probably English girls of the highest
classes have at this day more freedom of this kind,
more wholesome riding and rowing and tennis-playing
and mountain-scrambling than any young ladies ever
possessed before in any case or country. But even for
them senseless fashions of dress often interfere with
health and pleasure; while as they grow older the lesson
is too often enforced by their parents and governesses
and all their teachers and elder relations, that they
must put a curb,—*not* on their vanity and frivolity, *not*
on luxurious self indulgence,—but on their physical and
mental energy, their harmless animal spirits, their
righteous longing to be of some use in the world in
which they find themselves. To be content smilingly
to lie on a bed of roses while they know that thousands
around them sleep on thorns,—this is represented by
all around them as constituting pretty nearly the
"Whole Duty of Woman." Thus practising meekly
an aimless and unmeaning patience and self repression,
they dwindle down year by year into pettiness and
inanity.

Nor is it only *negative* evil, the loss of the potential
happiness intended for them, which women thus endure.
The positive suffering entailed on our sex by purely
artificial restrictions of one kind or other is far worse.

1 *

Among the upper classes there are maladies and weaknesses innumerable directly due to lack of healthful
interests in life, and to enforced obedience to hurtful
customs of dress ; and among the lower classes of women
there are other diseases due to excessive toil under the
conditions of their married lives, and to lack of proper
nourishment, which their ill-paid labour cannot earn.
Hard as poverty often presses on men, it is rare
indeed that they ever feel its iron grip as do
women, for whom so few fields of industry are open ;
and it must never be forgotten that hunger and want
for women imply the dread temptation, unknown to
men, to earn money only too readily by the sin which
leads them down headlong into the abyss of misery
and shame. When we think of all this as the outcome in great measure of artificial weights added to
their natural inferiority in the race of life, and then of
the wives trampled on by husbands whom the law has
taught to regard them as inferior beings ; * of the
mothers whose children are torn from their arms
by the direct behest of the law at the bidding of a
dead or living father ;—when we think of these things,

---

* According to the Returns it appears that there are in
England, on an average four, "aggravated assaults " by husbands
on wives every day in the year, counting alone the cases brought
before magistrates. An " aggravated assault" means a great
deal more than a simple blow. It means knocking out an eye,
" clogging" with hob-nailed boots (*i.e.* kicking or standing on
the woman), setting her on fire, breaking her ribs, throwing
a paraffin lamp at her, etc. etc.

as I have said, our hearts ache with pity and indignation.

But dreadful as they are, I believe that even these again are not the worst evils which women endure in consequence of their false position. I think it is worse to be poor in mind than poor in purse, to be stunted and be-littled in soul, made a coward, made a liar, made mean and slavish, accustomed to fawn and prevaricate, and "manage" by base arts a husband or a father—I think this is worse than to be kicked with hob-nailed shoes.

And yet again, what has not the whole human race lost by the degradation of women?

Of all the precious things in this arid world, love, tenderness, sympathy, are immeasurably the best; and the very fountain of such feelings is in woman's breast. It is the "compassion of a woman for the son of her womb," *the potential Motherhood* in every true woman's heart, which has been the great softening influence gradually through the ages melting the hardness and selfishness of savage humanity. But what narrow bounds have been placed by the claustration of women on the exercise of this divine power, aye, and of many another power, to guide and heal and bless!

At last, after long ages, there seems to be a great change coming over the destiny of women. Looking back to the past we seem dimly to perceive that the lot of our sex has passed through three stages.

First there was the *Savage Age,* where woman was
everywhere (as she is still among Red Indians) a mere
beast of burden, the camel or ass of her master, *plus*
the endurance, with or without her choice, of the pains
of motherhood.

Secondly, out of the early civilizations of India and
Greece, of the Teutonic and Scandinavian Nations,
and very notably of Judæa, there seems to have arisen
strangely enough an *Heroic Age* for women, when
they were not only as free as they now are in England,
but specially honoured. In the days of the Vedas in
India, and many centuries later, when the great
Buddhist Topes were built, we find, from the poetry
of the former and the bas-reliefs of the latter, that
women mixed freely and unveiled at feasts and sacrifices; and the two great Sanscrit epics, the Mahabhar-
ata and the Ramayuna, with some of the later tragedies,
turn on chivalrous stories wherein women play noble
parts and are nobly beloved—stories which it would
seem no modern Hindoo, with his degraded ideas of
womanhood, can properly understand.

In Greece again, as every one will recollect, the
Homeric age saw such women as Penelope, Andro-
mache, Nausicaa, Clytemnestra; and the tradition went
down for four centuries, till Sophocles, writing in the
time of the poor imprisoned wives of Periclean Athens,
yet looked back to the old heroic time, and created
such glorious types of womanhood as Alcestis and
Antigone.   The latter (I must be pardoned for pausing

for a moment to note), is the embodiment of the very highest moral ideal, masculine or feminine: namely, obedience to a Divine Law when it involves the penalty of death for disobeying a human law. To me it is one of the most wonderful facts in the literature of the world that Sophocles, living when he did, put into the mouth of a *woman* that most magnificent speech of Antigone concerning the "Unwritten Law Divine, immutable, eternal, not like these of yesterday, but made ere Time began." Again, the Hebrews had their Heroic Age of Women, when Miriam and Deborah were the types of that strength and courage which King Lemuel afterwards described as his ideal of a noble woman, " She strengtheneth her arms—she girdeth her loins with strength."*

And lastly, not to dwell too long on this bright gleam, falling on the dreary lot of women in one far-off epoch, there was the well known Heroic Age of Women among the Britons and Germans—the age to which Boadicea belonged, and of which Tacitus wrote when he said that the Germans thought that the minds of women were nearer to the Deity than those of men, and therefore they were always consulted with respect.

But the clouds gathered everywhere over this sunrise—why or wherefore in each country it boots not

---

* See a most remarkable paper on this subject, " The Hebrew Woman," by Mrs. Cyril Flower (Miss Constance de Rothschild) reprinted from the *New Quarterly Magazine*. (Hazell, Watson and Viney, London and Aylesbury, pp. 48.)

to inquire. There arose, I suppose, with the growth of luxury, a loss on the woman's side of the sterner virtues, and on that of men an increase of jealous and selfish passion and sense of proprietorship; and then followed throughout all the East and South, the miserable *Claustration* of women, their sequestration in their separate portions of the house, their banishment from all social pleasures of the other sex, the enforcement of veils, the employment of eunuchs as guardians, and in China, the last extremity of all, the deliberate crippling of the feet of every woman belonging to the higher classes.

This degradation of women, as we all know, never prevailed in the West and North to the extent it has done in the East and South. Whether Christianity alone has been the influence which saved women from it, I have my doubts, seeing that the Christian races of the Levant to this day keep their women in almost Mahometan seclusion, while the German races, whose women were free in the heathen days of Tacitus, have been neither more nor less free under Catholic or Protestant Christianity. The *character* of the women of each race seems to have more to do with the matter than any form of religion. The woman who is the slave of her own passions is everywhere the slave of man—the woman whose moral nature is supreme over her passions everywhere obtains a certain modicum of freedom. Nothing, alas! explains a Harem so well as a little acquaintaince with the half animal-natured women who are shut up in one of them.

The Harem has made them what they are, and their ungoverned passions afford an excuse for maintaining the Harem.

But if the women of Europe have never sunk entirely to the *ab*jection of the women of the East, they have suffered a *sub*jection severe and stringent enough. I shall not dwell on this painful subject. We are come here to think of our Duties, not of our Wrongs. The best and healthiest way to view all the huge injustices of the past, all the many lingering injustices of the present under which our sex has suffered, is to consider that men (even good and generous men) have treated women uniformly as *Minors*—sometimes as petted children, sometimes in the harsh and despotic way in which children were commonly treated in former days, but in any case making *obedience* a virtue in a wife of forty as it is in a child at four or fourteen, and compliance with their masterful wishes pretty nearly the be-all and end-all of the virtue of a woman, as it is of a dog or a baby.

Now it would seem at last we are on the point of attaining our majority! An immense wave is lifting up women all over the world, and if we " survey *womankind* from China to Peru " we shall find in almost every country of the globe (by no means excepting Japan) a new demand for education, for domestic freedom, and for civil and political rights, made by women on behalf of their sex.

I need not detain you by citing all the steps which have been already gained, all which we hope to gain

ere long. When women of my age look back on the
state of things which prevailed in our youth, we seem
to have passed under a *New Dispensation* *

There can be no doubt that a great change is passing
over the condition of women everywhere in the civilized world. That is not our concern at this moment,
but it is our most vital concern to consider how far
that great change is likely to be a benefit to our sex
and to both sexes. That it *will* be an immense benefit
I suppose most of us here present are persuaded.
But can we close our eyes to the possibility that it
may prove otherwise? Is it not a contingency that
so much disorder, so many disgraceful failures, such a
pitiful fulfilment of our large promises may come,
and so many now common womanly virtues be
lost without the attainment of any other moral
gifts or graces—that, fifty years hence, our epoch
will be looked back upon as a disastrous one, and
either our reforms be all reformed back again, and the
status quo ante restored, or else a state of things
inaugurated which we should weep to think we had
helped to bring about?

---

* Only seventen years ago I myself read a paper in Guildhall,
at the Social Science Congress, pleading for the admission of
women to University Degrees, and every newspaper in London
laughed at me (notably our now most friendly *Spectator*), for
asking for what would *never* be granted! Two years ago, when
I had the honour to go up on a deputation to Lord Granville
to thank him for this very admission of women to London
University, I placed in his hands, to his amusement, my much
ridiculed Address.

I confess that I see numberless threatening rocks
ahead. One of them is a growth of hardness and of
selfishness among women as their lives cease to be
a perpetual self-oblation, and they (very properly)
pursue ends of their own. Another is the occurrence
of much social disorder before there is time for a
new code of *bienséances* to be formed, and before
the ultimate laws of the relations of the sexes have
themselves been first called in question, and are then
(as I believe they will be), re-established in the
morality of the future much the same as we find
them now. There are in fact dangers all round us.
The entrance obtained into the Medical profession is a
danger. It is *possible* there may arise such a monster
as a woman vivisector, a female Schiff, or Bernard,
though, thank God, as yet there are little signs of
such ignominy.

Here, as in many other directions, as I have said,
there are rocks ahead. Our course towards a free and
ennobled womanhood is by no means a secure and safe
one, nor should we altogether condemn those amongst
us who see these dangers more clearly than the advan-
tages we promise, and deprecate the changes to which
we look so hopefully.

What is it which must determine whether this great
change, fraught with such infinite consequences to
humanity, will be a benefit or an injury, a blessing or
a curse? It must be the *conduct of women themselves
during the great transition*. Nothing our opponents

can do or say—nothing which all *men* united together
could do—would really determine the character and
results of the revolution. It must be our work, the
way we pass through the process of emancipation, the
tone we adopt, the principles we choose to guide us.

Here is the point to which I am bringing you. It
depends on the ideas of DUTY held by the women of
our time, and their faithfulness to those ideas, whether
we shall enter into an era of true progress, wherein
our sex shall not only be infinitely happier but infinitely nobler, infinitely more useful than it has ever
been; or whether, after a brief blaze of promise, our
hopes are destined to die and end in bitterest shame
and disappointment.

And what women are they on whose ideas and conduct so much must depend ? Pre-eminently it must be,
at least so far as Europe is concerned, the women of
England,—and among these necessarily the women of
the upper classes, the intellectual women, the women
who take part in the movements of progress, and
whose example will affect those who follow. I fail
to find words to say how important it seems to me
that at this crisis of woman's history every one of us
should, each in our small way, begin to tread the new
path carefully, giving no just cause of reproach, or
scandal, or ridicule; but, on the contrary, making the
way for all who come after us plainer and easier; and
always *in the right direction*, in the direction not only
of a larger and freer life, but of a life of higher self-

reverence, broader piety, more tender goodness, purer purity, truer truth.

Does any one think we are either going to fling aside *all* the old moral restraints, or, on the other hand, that we can *keep* them all just as they have been under the new order of things? Both ideas are absurd. The eternal principles of morality must bind us for ever, but the application of those principles to practical duties must be revised and reconsidered as the conditions of life are altered, just as the duties of a boy and of a man are different. Women, as I have said before, have hitherto been treated as *Minors*, and have been taught the duties of Minors,—unquestioning obedience and a child-like ductility. Now they are to be *Human Beings of the Mother Sex* (that is the best definition I can find for them), and their duties must be *human*, including the whole circle of human virtues, and applying them to the special obligations of daughter, mother, wife,— a female member of Society and of the State.

Considerable care and thought it seems to me are needed to adjust all the problems of practical womanly life to this higher and truer view of woman's nature and obligations, and I wish that some one better fitted for it than I had first undertaken the task. However, as our clergy (though they preach occasionally both to Men and to Children) never seem inclined to tackle the subject of Woman's special duties (and, indeed, would perhaps generally lay them down on

principles which few of us here assembled would
altogether accept), it seems well that some woman
should commence the work ; and for lack of one better
qualified, I have attempted it with a very keen sense
of my own presumption in so doing.

It would occupy more than the time allotted for
this whole course of Lectures were I to preface them,
as would be otherwise desirable, by a statement of
the Theory of Morals on which I proceed, and some
exposure of the fallacies (as I conceive them to be) of
opposite systems. I must refer any of you who desire
to go further into this matter to my former treatises
on ethics,* and now briefly say that I assume those who
hear me to accept the following fundamental beliefs,
without which much which follows would be baseless.

First, I assume that you accept the fact that there is
such a thing as DUTY, and that it is supremely sacred.
Virtue is no empty dream, but the soundest of all
realities. *How we come by our sense* of Duty, *how we*

---

* In my *Essay on Intuitive Morals*, I have done what lay in
my power to work out a consistent Theory of Ethics, mainly on
the lines of Kant's " *Grundlegung der Sitten*," in harmony with
a definite Theism ; and in my " *Darwinism in Morals*," and the
preface to my " *Hopes of the Human Race*," I have explained
at length the reasons for my entire dissent from the doctrines of
the most recent school of moralists which trace our moral sense
to the inherited "set" of our brains,— the "capitalized
experience of our tribe " (as Mr. Martineau has happily expressed it)—affording us a slight prejudice in favour of honesty
and truth, and a certain distaste of cruelty and lies.

know what is our Duty; *how,* amid the coil of the
chain of phenomena we are enabled to exercise that
free choice of Duty wherein Virtue consists,—all these
questions which touch the deepest roots of human
thought, I must leave aside for the present. Let
it be enough that we recognize that there is a holy
Law demanding our obedience, and that we are
conscious of possessing the power to obey it, or to
disobey. These are postulates of which the acceptance is indispensable to any moral discussion.

Secondly, I assume that you believe in God and in a
life for the soul of man beyond the grave. These great
doctrines are not indeed like the former, absolutely
indispensable to the erection of a theory of morals, but
in the subsequent pages reference will be made to
them as accepted truths.

Thirdly, I assume that you will grant readily that
the Motive of Virtue must always be Virtue itself, and
not any ulterior reward here, or hereafter. The only
reward of a right action is to have done right; the
only reward of duty is to have done our duty; the only
reward of obedience to God is to have obeyed Him;
and (perhaps we may add) to have the better hope of
obeying Him for evermore.

These few points indicate the outline of a very old-
fashioned system of morals, which yet I should not
despair of entirely commending to your acceptance
were time enough at our disposal. For the present
you will please accept them at least provisionally,

as the scaffolding of the practical part of our subject which is to follow.

I have said the belief in God and Immortality are not absolutely indispensable to a system of morals. Morals may be separated from Religion, and it is quite possible to erect a general scheme of duty on the sole ground of the inherent necessary rightfulness of one class of actions and sentiments, and wrongfulness of another. For those, then, to whom in these sad days that Being whom our fathers well named the " Sun of Righteousness " is hidden behind a cloud of doubt, it is, I think, of inestimable value thus to be able to separate in thought the obligations of morality from any and every religious creed; and to recognize that Goodness remains good and noble and beautiful, and Evil remains base and hideous and abominable, and Virtue is still the law of the higher will, the true self of man,—even supposing it to be true that there is no One in all this dark universe in whom that goodness is impersonated, no Guide to lead our faltering steps in the right way, no Hope of a home beyond the grave where the poor struggling virtue of earth may ascend into the holiness and peace of Heaven.

It is well, I think, to recognize this possible separation, and very fit that we should honour those whom we see still marching resolutely along the thorny path of duty, even though they have lost the faiths which are like wings to the soul to bear it onward. But as, in my view, these doubters are in uttermost error,—as I believe that there is indeed a God, the Supreme All-Righteous Lord in whom we live and have our being now and with whom we shall live for ever after death—I cannot look upon the great laws of morals as dissociated from the idea of Him. On the contrary it seems to me that only with the sunlight of His presence illuminating our vision of the moral world do we obtain light on its dark places, and warmth to stir our hearts to self-sacrifice. It is when we think of the world as His Kingdom and of our brothers as His children, that we can love and labour with cheerfulness; and when we trust Him to do justice hereafter, we become able to endure the spectacle of the wrongs and cruelties which surround us now.

I shall not then waste the short time at our disposal by any attempt to delineate a system of Atheistic Morals; but rather turn to a doctrine of Theistic ethics, which I cannot ask you to accept without some further explanation, but which I earnestly hope you may be willing to adopt on reflection, seeing that it throws (in my humble judgment) a wide and glorious light over the whole moral horizon of humanity.

In the eyes of an all-righteous God who sees all the evil of evil, all the goodness of good, all the beauty and joy of a holy soul, and all the hideousness and misery of a sinful one,—everything else in the universe, all the pains and pleasures of this transitory life, all human hopes and ambitions must seem as dust in the balance compared to the supreme realities of the moral world. In His view there must be an absolutely boundless significance in the free choice between virtue and vice. All analogies known to us fail to express the difference between a holy and loving soul, and a soul wallowing in pollution and cruelty. Taking in the vast scope of our immortal existence, every other circumstance of our lives must to Him seem trivial as the toys of an infant. What then follows, but that supreme Benevolence must render the *virtue* of man, not his mere *happiness*, the goal of his destiny, the underlying purpose of all his education in this planet? I cannot doubt then, that in calling us into life, dowering us with the awful gift of moral responsibility, and placing us in a world of trial like this, our Creator has designed to lead us upward to the highest possible good of finite creatures—namely, to that Virtue which approaches ever nearer and nearer to divine holiness. The *End of Creation*, I believe to be the *perfecting of souls ;* the training in virtue of the human race (and doubtless of myriads of other intelligent races in other worlds) through a thousand lessons of struggle and effort, pain and pleasure, trial and temptation, into higher and yet higher moral conditions, wherein as we rise we shall come nearer to the Father of our spirits, enjoy more of His Communion, resemble Him more closely in purity, love and holiness, and at last be fitted to enjoy a bliss of Divine love and joy such as we cannot picture now, but which " God has prepared for them who love Him"; aye, and for those who as yet in their darkness love Him not, or know Him not.

This is, according to my faith, the 'Destiny of Man, the only Purpose of Creation which we can reverently attribute to a good and perfect God, and also the only one which, in a certain large and general way, affords some rough explanation of the sin and sorrow which surround us now. Accept then, again I beg of you— provisionally at least, while we thus confer on our duties,—this doctrine (or hypothesis if you will not admit it to be more), namely, that we are each of us made on purpose to attain, by the performance of duty and the fulfilment of God's will, a loftier stage of moral life than we have now reached, serving as a step up an endless stair upon whose higher flights above the clouds of earth and sin we shall find unbroken communion with God and the fulness of eternal joy.

We have advanced so far towards treating of the Duties of Women, that we have reached the broad ground of the duties common to all moral beings in all worlds for ever—namely, to choose the right and eschew the wrong wheresoever there may be a right and wrong betwixt which choice is possible.* Now

---

* The oldest text in the oldest part of the Zend Avesta (the Gatha Ahunavaiti, believed to be the address of Zoroaster himself at the inauguration of his mission), runs thus :—" There are two spirits; the good and the base. Be good and not base!" We shall never see the day wherein those words do not

2 *

assuming this broad standpoint of universal morality,
we see manifestly that all virtues must be really alike
for all moral agents. It is only the *field in which the
virtues are to be exercised* by Marcus Aurelius or
Epictetus, by prince or slave, by the old man or the
boy, the rich or the poor, the man or the woman,
nay, if there be such creatures, by Archangels, and by
you and me,—in which there can be any difference. The
highest is not above, nor the lowest below, the simple
universal obligation to *do the right* whenever there is
a right and a wrong between which to choose. And
the choice of right in each department of life and
conduct is the exercise of the special virtue belonging
to that department. To choose right speech when a
lie is convenient, is the virtue of *veracity*. To choose
right dealings is the virtue of *justice*. To choose to bear
any suffering rather than do wrong is the virtue of
courage—and so on through the whole round of morals.
This must sound to many of you as a mere truism and
platitude, but my experience convinces me that it is
not superfluous repeatedly to affirm that virtue is
essentially *the same thing* for every moral being, and
among moral beings for a man and for a woman. Thus

contain the core of morals and religion. I am not sure that I do
not prefer the word rendered "base," to "bad," or its theo-
logical anologue "sinful." Every vice or wrong doing, be it
the "scarlet sin" itself, the domination of the wills and lives of
others, or ungoverned passion of any kind, is essentially and
supereminently *base.*"

we recognize that in speaking of the duties of women, we are not concerned with a different *set of virtues* from those of Men-Heroes and Men-Saints, but with just the same virtues exercised in a somewhat different field. We learn to bear in mind that whatever be the aim and end of the creation of a Man—the end which he ought steadfastly to contemplate and towards which he should guide the whole voyage of his life,—that *same* aim and end is ours, and we too must keep it prominently before our eyes. I think we women have reason to thank Milton for having so distinctly and lucidly set forth the opposite and prevailing error— the great moral *heresy* (as I reckon it) on this point, so that we can recognize it in a moment and renounce it distinctly. Milton's doctrine, as you all know, is, that Man only is made directly for God's service ;

"*He* for God only—*she* for God in him,"

or, as he elsewhere makes Eve say to Adam—

"God is thy law—thou mine !"

Now, if we women are to advance one step forward, our very first leap must be over this abominable and ridiculous doctrine ! For once in my life I find myself able to avail myself of the words of the Westminster Catechism, and I say that we are made "to know God and enjoy Him for ever," to live for Him and make ourselves like Him, and advance His kingdom, which means the reign of justice, truth, and love—and all this directly and immediately, and not for God " *in* " any man alive.

Here is the root of the misplacement of women, that they have been deemed by men, and have contentedly deemed themselves, to have only a secondary purpose in the order of things. Brigham Young's doctrine that only a woman *sealed* to a man in marriage can possibly be saved, is little more than a carrying out of our British legislator's idea, that women who do not marry (and so do not immediately contribute to the comfort of some particular man) are " *Failures.*" They have no *raison d'être* in creation, any more I suppose, than the mistletoe without the apple-tree ! The Hindoos formerly carried out this idea to its logical conclusion by suttee. When the man died, it was time to burn the widow. When we cut down the tree, the mistletoe dies. Of course there is a sense in which every created being is made for others. Creation is like one of those vast Suspension bridges in which every bar and chain tends to support the whole structure. But in *this* sense man also is made for woman, the father for the son, the daughter for the mother, and so on *ad infinitum*. There is no degradation to any, but honour to all, in this view of the solidarity of the family, the State and Humanity. And why ? Because every one recognizes that it is only the secondary purpose of each to help the other. The primary *raison d'être* of every one is his own existence, and only in a secondary sense he exists for others. As Tennyson beautifully says in the grandest lines in " In Memoriam," his faith is that—

> " Not a moth with vain desire
> Shall shrivel in a fruitless fire,
> *Or but subserve another's gain.*"

Even the poor moth cannot be contemplated as only " subserving " another !

Let us take it once for all thoroughly to heart. We women have before us the noblest end to which a finite creature may attain; and our duty is nothing else than the fulfilment of the whole moral law, the attainment of every human virtue.

How shall we now, for our present purposes, map out this vast field of morality ? Necessarily I must do it merely in outline that we may pass on to the more special subjects of these addresses.

Practical Morality includes three branches of Duty : RELIGIOUS DUTY, PERSONAL DUTY, and SOCIAL DUTY. All Duties are, in one sense, Religious. We owe it to God to lift our souls up to the blessed end of union with Himself for which He has created us; and we owe it to Him to love and serve our fellow men who are His children, and to be kind to the brutes which are His creatures. But in speaking here of Religious Duty as a branch of ethics, I refer to the special Duties owed *directly* by man to God, whenever he recognizes that there is above him such a Being, his Creator and Benefactor, the Lord of Conscience, the absolutely Holy One, the Alpha and Omega of his existence.

"Path, Motive, Guide, Original and End."

These, strictly speaking, RELIGIOUS DUTIES may be classified under the heads of *Thanksgiving, Repentance, Prayer, Faith, Adoration,* and *Self-Consecration,* and may be summed up in the canon "Thou shalt love the Lord thy God."

The second branch of Morals is PERSONAL DUTY, the duty directly concerning ourselves, the pursuit of the proper End of our being; inward rather than outward virtue; *being* good as distinguished from *doing* good. These Personal Duties may be classified under the heads of *Chastity, Temperance, Veracity, Courage,* and the conservation of our *Freedom* (whereby alone any other duty can be performed). They may be summed up in the canon "Be Perfect."

The third branch of Morals is SOCIAL DUTY, the Duty which concerns all our fellow creatures. These duties may be classified in various ways; in these Lectures we shall treat them in order as regards the objects of each Duty, viz.—Duties of the Family; Duties of the Household; of Society; and of the State. All these Social Duties may be summed up by the canon "Thou shalt love thy Neighbour as Thyself."

Now of this great trinity of human duties, Religious, Personal, and Social, we need not concern ourselves in these lectures with the first, seeing that no one in Christian countries has been silly enough to suggest that there is any difference between the Religious Duties of a man and those of a woman— unless indeed, it be that a religious man is bidden to let his "light shine before men that they may glorify his Father in Heaven," while a woman is generally counselled to place *her* Divine light carefully under a bushel !

There remain PERSONAL and SOCIAL Duty for our consideration, and the first thing to be done is to determine their relative rank in the hierarchy of moral obligations, so that if they ever *seem* to clash (they cannot really do so) we may know at once which of the two possesses the first claim on our obedience.

Do not be shocked or startled if I lay it down as an unquestionable principle that Personal Duties have supreme obligation and must *never* be postponed to Social ones. I must explain this doctrine, fully.

We hear a great deal of Social Duty in these days under the name of *Altruism*; and, as much of the philosophy of the hour has relegated God to the land of shadows and cut off from man that hope of Immortality which gives to virtue its infinite extension, it follows of course that Social Duty must come to be considered as the supreme and only real moral obligation, and even the most sacred Personal Duties end in being ranked and estimated according to the influence they happen to exercise on the welfare of the community.

I cannot too strenuously express my dissent from this entire view of morality. As I believe that *Virtue* is a far higher thing—a more desirable thing even to the weakest of us, than *Happiness,* so (as I have just said) I believe that we have been *made* primarily for Virtue, and only secondarily, and as far as may be compatible with our primary end, for Happiness,—and I cannot listen to the base theory of human existence which makes of such things as Truth, and Purity, and Holiness of Heart, only convenient characteristics tending generally to make the community in which they abound a little more orderly and comfortable. On the contrary, I believe that the individual himself—the community itself—the very material world itself,—all exist for the purpose that human spirits may rise through the paths of mortal excellence up into loftier regions of purity, love and holiness, to a beatitude compared to which our poor *Happiness* of earth will be utterly forgotten.

Therefore I hold that whenever Personal and Social Duties seem to come into collision, the Personal Duty must have the precedence. We must not sacrifice our Truthfulness, and Chastity, and Temperance, in the vain hope of benefiting our neighbours, for

these two plain reasons; first, because, as Virtue is
the true end of our being, and we can only choose
virtue for ourselves and not for another, and can never
make anybody else virtuous (only in an indirect way
help him to virtue), it follows that it is absurd to
postpone our own virtue to any lesser object. And,
secondly, because we can never really benefit anybody
by doing wrong on his behalf, and the truest and
surest way in which we can serve our fellow men is,
not so much to *do* anything for them, as to *be* the very
truest, purest, noblest beings we know how. This is I
fear, a hard lesson to take to heart, and you will pardon
me if, in addressing women, I dwell on it specially
because I think it is a matter on which the most
generous natured women are most apt to err. There
have been hundreds of women who, like Judith of old,
or like the piteous poverty-stricken mother in "Les
Miserables," will sacrifice their chastity to serve their
race or their children. There are thousands, tens of
thousands of women who, like the wife of "Auld
Robin Gray," have made unloving marriages (which
are in truth, though not in name, unchaste likewise)
to aid their parents in distress, and even to gratify
their wishes. And again, there are thousands of
women (and of men also) who are ready to sacrifice
their veracity to do charitable actions; to conceal
some one's faults, or help some one to employment;
and in short, to bear false witness *for* their neighbours
—the reverse of the noble and sweet examples of

Jeannie Deans and Mary Barton. And lastly there are
millions of women throughout the world whose freedom
is wholly robbed from them, and who for all moral
purposes are little better than slaves, and who submit
patiently to this under the notion that it is a duty
to husband or father. Now on every one of these
kinds of *self*-oblations the same sentence must be
passed. They are mistakes,—often generous, affecting, heart-rending mistakes — but always mistakes.
No good can ever come of them. The highest
ends of human life are spoiled by them, and the
benefit they aim at is never worth that which is
forfeited. *

---

* The following story was told to me by the gentleman to whom
it happened. He had a butler who fell into habits of intoxication. After threatening him several times with dismissal, the
gentleman was compelled, after a very gross case of drunkenness,
to send him away. The man implored him to give him a
character which would enable him to obtain another place, but
this Mr. S. conscientiously refused to do. Time after time the
butler was on the point of obtaining employment, but was
rejected when the silence of his late master on the matter of
sobriety betrayed the reasons for his dismissal. At last the
man, much impoverished and driven to the wall, wrote a piteous
letter to Mr. S. vowing that if he would but once recommend
him, he would take the pledge ; and adding that if he refused,
he had resolved to make an end of himself, as he had no further
hope of earning his bread. The master was greatly disturbed
by this appeal, and only by most painful effort held to his duty
of veracity ; for weeks afterwards fearing in every newspaper
to read of some tragedy connected with his unfortunate servant.
Years, however, passed before he heard of him again, and
then he received a letter from Australia. The ex-butler had

No my friends, it is a mere truism, but at the same time a profound truth to say, "It can never be right to do wrong." It is not even right to *suffer* one kind of wrong—that is the wrong which robs us of our sacred birthright of moral Freedom. The only remaining fragment of the apocryphal Gospel of St. Bartholomew contains this extraordinary text : " If the neighbour of an elect person sin, half the guilt of the sin belongs to the elect person, for if he had displayed before him the beauty of holiness he would not have sinned." Making allowance for Eastern hyperbole, there is here a great truth. If we could but thoroughly reflect the Divine goodness in our hearts we should be as moons in the sky of mortal night. We all *catch* goodness and piety and love from one another, or on the contrary *catch* corruption and cruelty, in a much more direct way than we receive any influence from mere acts or words. It is the *living man* or woman, himself or herself, who lifts us up or drags us down, and in whose " sphere " (as the Swedenborgians say) we are elevated and purified, or polluted and degraded ; made nobler, larger by the one, or *be-littled* by the other. All

---

become a prosperous and sober man, and wrote to *thank* his old master for the firmness wherewith he had refused his entreaty. " Had you sent me Sir," he said, " to another place, I should have fallen again under the same temptation. You compelled me to break away from my old life, and I was saved."

the greatest heroes and prophets and saints of history
have influenced mankind far more by what they *were,*
than by what they said or did.   The whole moral life
of the further East has been coloured by the mind
and heart of Gautama Buddha ; and the stupendous
change which has passed over humanity during the
last eighteen hundred years and which we name Christianity, has had for its mainspring (acting to this hour
through millions of hearts), not so much the Sermon
on the Mount, or even the martyrdom of Calvary,
as the *personal character* of Jesus Christ.

Now you will please cast a glance back over the
outline of Practical Morals we have just sketched :—

1. RELIGIOUS DUTY ; summed up in the Love of God.
Of this we shall say no more at present.

2. PERSONAL DUTY; summed up in the Lifting of
our own souls to God and goodness.

3. SOCIAL DUTY; summed up in the Love of our
Neighbour.

The next Lecture will be devoted to the consideration of *Personal Duty,* with special regard to its
bearing on the life of Women and to the mistakes
which prevail among women concerning it.   The four
subsequent Lectures will be concerned with *Social
Duty,* in its ever widening circles from the Family to
the Household, from the Household to Society, and
from Society to the State and the World.

In conclusion, my friends, let me appeal to you if you have not hitherto thought of these great lessons of morals in the light in which I have endeavoured to place them, and if now they strike you as true and right,—to take to heart practically what has been said about our *human* rank and our *human* duties. A great living teacher once made to me the curious observation that he had noticed that when a woman was persuaded that anything was right or true she generally tried to shape her conduct and creed accordingly. But (he added with comic despair), " when I have, as I think, entirely convinced a *man* in the same way and expect to see some results of his conviction, behold ! he goes on precisely as he did before, and as if nothing had happened." Now will you not take heart of grace and thus act up, *womanlike*, to any convictions which I may have been happy enough to bring to you, and evermore henceforth bear in mind that you are not *first women*, and then, perhaps, rational creatures ; but first of all *human beings* and then, secondly, women,— human beings of the mother-sex ?

Let me, if I may without presumption, speak to the young ones among you, as a woman who has borne somewhat of the battle and heat of the day. Awake to recognize your true rank in creation, your noble destination. Laugh at the doctrine that you are a sort of moon, with no *raison d'être* but to go circling round and round a very earthy planet ; or a kind of parasite,— ivy, or honeysuckle in the forest. You *may* be,—you probably *are* less strong, less clever, less rich, and less well-educated than most of the men about you.   But moral rank does not depend on these things. You are a rational free agent, a child of God, destined to grow nearer to Him and more like Him through the ages of your immortality. As such you are the equal (*ebenwur-dig,* as people say of royal alliances) with the loftiest of created beings, not one of whom can have a higher destiny.   Cast then aside, for shame's sake, the faults and follies which have accumulated round our woman-hood through the long centuries of the *minority* of our sex.   Little girls may fitly play with toys, and dress dolls, and chatter in the nursery for hours over some weighty concern of the baby-house; but it is a pitiful sight to see grown women making all life a child's play.   Rise, I pray you, to the true dignity of a human being to whom petty feelings and small vanities and servile wheedling tricks must be repugnant and abominable.   Respect yourself too much to dress like a doll or a peacock, or to betray that you must have spent hours in devising the trimming of a gown.   And respect other women also, and never join men in sneering at the deplorable weaknesses which have followed from their wretched circumstances and educa-tion.   When I see in the street a poor threadbare broken-spirited woman, wearing that peculiar look of patient, hopeless endurance which belongs to women only, to trodden-down wives or starving widows, my heart aches for the hapless creature.

But when I see another woman, healthy and prosperous as the world goes, abasing herself to the mean
artifices and cajolings, the wheedlings and subterfuges
which some wives use to manage their husbands, when
I hear her tell lies to her lord and master to avert his
wrath or to hide from him her most innocent actions,
then my heart burns with indignation, not so much
against the woman herself, as against the dead weight
of life-long oppression which has warped her into this
pitiful, superannuated school girl. I cannot laugh at
these things. I cannot heap scorn on such women. I
scorn too much the whole theory of woman's life which
has made them what they are.

I know it is a difficult thing to keep in mind the
true dignity of our womanhood in face of the deep
underlying sentiment of something like contempt (or
let us call it, *disprezzo*) wherewith all but the most
generous of men regard us. Sometimes it would seem
as if the conventional courtesy and excessive outward
show of respect wherewith every gentleman treats a
lady, adds the sting of irony to the consciousness we
feel that, at bottom, nine out of ten of these bowing
and smiling acquaintances think our whole sex unfit to
exercise the smallest political right, or indeed to entertain a political or religious opinion which it might be
worth their while to weigh against a feather. Of
course the origin of this *disprezzo* is not far to seek.
From a child a man has seen women debarred by law
from the exercise of those functions to which he is to

3

be admitted at the outset of manhood; and he has too often furthermore seen his father treat his mother's judgment about business of all kinds as if he were condescending to let her talk on matters of which the ultimate decision must always rest with the nobler sex. The very same men who will indite most affecting things in prose and verse about the sacred influence of a mother, and tell us that that of a good mother over her son is something quite divine, those same men do their very worst by incessantly snubbing and setting down their wives and treating their opinions as of no consequence, to reduce this " sacred influence " to a minimum. It is all very well to teach a boy in his catechism to " honour his mother" as well as his father. But when he comes to find that his mother is classified by the constitution of his country along with Criminals, Idiots, Lunatics and Minors—is it likely he will honour her ?

Of course there is no need to assume affected gravity or to become a moral *prig* by way of asserting our dignity. On the contrary, affectation of all kinds is a contemptible foible which does our sex infinite damage, whether it be the affectation of timidity and overstrained modesty common twenty years ago, or the newer fashion of affectation of "fastness" and mannishness in dress and habits. It must be from our inward sense that must radiate the true behaviour of dignified humanity. And this true dignity is attainable by every woman, young or old, rich or poor, clever or simple.

Many of us necessarily lead, what seem to outsiders, small and narrow lives. We are poor, (alas! how many women, even those living in splendid homes, are miserably shackled in the use of a few pounds or shillings!) many of us have feeble health, and very limited powers of any sort. But all this need not interfere with real dignity of character. People go on repeating George Herbert's wonderful line:

> " Who sweeps a room as for *Thy* laws
> Makes that, and the action fine."

but they do not note how it covers the whole meaning of homely lives. She who does everything " as for God's laws " brings an element of beauty, nay, of true *greatness* into the very humblest mortal lot.

It is a vast responsibility which lies on us, my friends, to do whatever may be in our power to lift up the Womanhood of the Future, to reclaim it from the faults, and save it from the shame and suffering of the past, and to help on our whole sex to lead diviner lives; lives more blessed for themselves, and assuredly also more blessed for men, than women have yet led in any age or country. Progress, Civilization, Christianity will only have done their work when this is achieved. Men can only be truly civilized and Christianized when women are free and ennobled; and women can only be truly emancipated when men are moralized and purified. The two " rise and fall together " as our poet-philosopher Tennyson says so truly. He who labours to lift Woman labours in the

3 *

most effectual way to lift Man. He who does most
to cure woman of her weakness, her frivolity and her
servility, will likewise at the same stroke do most to
cure man of his brutality, his selfishness and his
sensuality. The human race can only advance, like the
human body, by the joint motion of *both* its limbs.

But if this rising tide of womanly energy and
freedom should indeed lift us permanently, if, as I
fervently hope and believe, we are at the beginning
of a new era for our sex and for the world, then how
immeasurably important it is that we should each
and all take profoundly to heart the seriousness of our
womanly duty, the heavy obligation which rests on us
to do all we can to direct this great movement aright
and to make it the blessing it ought to be, and not a
failure and a calamity! I know no better way to do
this than to cast behind us the faults and follies of the
past, and rise to meet our brighter, nobler destiny,—
even, my friends, as we would rise up in a church
to join a hymn of praise,—*and prayer.*

LECTURE II.

———◆———

Personal Duty.

IN our last discussion we classified human duty under three heads, RELIGIOUS DUTY, PERSONAL DUTY, and SOCIAL DUTY.

The wide and deep topic of *Religious Duty* we leave aside in this Course. No one in Christian lands holds that a woman's duties of Prayer, Thanksgiving, Repentance, Faith, &c., towards God, differ from those of a man. The books devoted to such themes are equally addressed to both sexes.*

The second great branch of Duty, *Personal Duty,* is the subject of our present consideration. In the last lecture you will remember, we advanced so far as to rank these duties above Social Duties. In other words, whenever it would appear that a Personal Duty (such as Chastity or Veracity) clashes with a Social Duty (such as Benevolence), the Personal Duty must

---

* If any reader should care to learn the author's views on this subject, they will be found in a volume entitled "*Religious Duty,*" 1 vol. 8vo. 2nd edition, *Williams and Norgate.*

at all hazards, be chosen. It is for example, an
offence to bear false witness *in favour* of our neighbour, as well as *against* him.

An inquiry into the grounds and reasons why each
special personal virtue holds its place in morals,
would carry us far, indeed, beyond the limits of these
Lectures. Very interesting, and also very lofty views,
on the subject, may be found by those who may care
to go deeply into it, in Kant's Metaphysic of Ethics.
All that I can here afford to do, is to mark those
features of personal character which will be admitted
by every one to constitute that Moral Perfection, which
is the aim of existence for a rational free agent. I
think no hesitation will be felt in granting that this
ideal of moral perfection includes the following five
Virtues—or, as we may express it, the fulfilment of
these five Duties:—*Chastity, Temperance, Veracity,
Courage,* and the *Vindication of rightful Liberty.*

Merely to contemplate the opposite vices, is enough
to satisfy us that any one of them must cast down the
soul from the heights of its upward flight to the very
mire of earth; and that neither the unchaste person,
nor the drunkard, nor the liar, nor the coward, nor
the voluntary slave, can be fulfilling the purpose of
his existence, or ascending towards the Divine ideal.
It is, however, a very poor and inadequate conception
of any Virtue, which we form when we think of it
only as the antithesis of the opposite vice, the *negation*
of the corresponding evil. On the contrary, I beg you

will carry with you through all our future discussions, both of Personal and Social Duties, the invigorating thought that Virtue is the *positive* thing, and Vice the *negative*. Both etymologically and philosophically, *Wrong* means "*wrung from*" the Right. It is no less unscientific to say "Whatever is not wrong is right," than to say "Whatever is not cold is heat." In each case the truth is that the "negative of right is wrong;" the "negative of caloric is cold." It may seem to some of you that this distinction is a mere logical quibble, but it has, I am deeply persuaded, vast practical importance. So long as we look on right as the mere absence of wrong, we can never comprehend its affirmative importance and essential vitality. To "do no harm" is the extent of our moral ambition, not "*do* good and *be* good." In the dawn of morality it was inevitable that the first thing perceived was the turpitude of the worst kinds of offences; and accordingly, the Hebrew and Buddhist Decalogues, and the forty-two Commandments of the Egyptian "Book of the Dead," are nearly exclusively negative. Do *not* Murder, Do *not* steal, and so on. It is one of the supreme characteristics of the teachings of Christ, that he converted the negative Mosaic commandments into the positive Christian law. "Thou *shalt* love the Lord thy God—Thou *shalt* love thy neighbour." The Rabbins had long before had a Golden Rule (attributed to Rabbi Hillel of the Babylonish captivity), "What ever you would *not* wish your neighbour to do to you, do it not to him. This is the law, the rest is only an exposition of it." Christ said (Matt. vi. 12), "Therefore whatever you *would* that men should do unto you, do ye even so unto them, for this is the law and the prophets."*

Virtue then, the free choice of Duty, you will please always to bear in mind is here understood to be the *affirmative*, the *positive*, thing. To *fail* in the performance of a duty is, in strict ethical language, a FAULT. To do that which is the opposite of the duty, is an OFFENCE.

Let us now turn to consider these various Personal Duties, the sum of which perfectly fulfilled would constitute Personal Virtue. Regarding them from our particular standpoint in these lectures on the Duties of Women, I suppose almost every one here present will be struck by the fact that some of them seem to have been set apart by public opinion for the practice of women, and others for the practice of men. The *honour* of each sex is supposed to be involved only in maintaining its particular virtues; Chastity and Temperance for Women, and Veracity and Courage for men,—and neither is supposed to be essentially disgraced by failing in the virtues of the other. It is difficult to find words to express how absurd is this

---

* The same maxim in its negative form is to be found in Isocrates (in Nicoc), and in both its negative and positive form in the "Yun Lu" of Confucius.—Maxim, 24.

idea,—as if the perfect human being, either man or woman, must not unite all the virtues, and as if the opposite vices were not equally dishonourable and degrading for either the one sex or the other! The matter is too grave for a jest, but as I have thought of how to illustrate the abject folly and stupidity of the prevailing view, nothing better has occurred to me than the old Joe Miller story of the two Irishmen who set off to walk from Charing Cross to Hampstead Heath, and asked a neighbour " What was the distance ?" " About four miles," was the reply. " Ah, then," said the Irishmen, cheerfully setting off, " as there are *two* of us to get there, it is only *two miles apiece !*" Whenever you hear of honourable men who are only courageous and truthful, and not chaste and temperate, or of virtuous women who are chaste and temperate but are cowards and liars, I beg you will bear this little parable in mind,—They have set out to walk to Hampstead, and think it is only two miles apiece !

Notice also the pleasant compromise by which the easiest duties for each have been chosen by the sexes for their respective *chevaux de bataille*. It is small praise to any woman to say she is temperate and chaste. To feel any inclination to be otherwise is already a disgrace. And in the same way it is no special honour to a man to be courageous and to speak the truth. The natural boldness and combativeness which we see in all male animals should suffice to make

his bravery and veracity innate and mere matters of
temperament. As Aristotle justly says, such virtues,
and also generosity, ought always to be spontaneous
and not acquired with effort. But for a woman to be
courageous and true, and for a man to curb his passions
and be chaste and temperate, is really praiseworthy
and honourable, and should accordingly be the ground
of respect,—the point of honour for each sex; and
not *vice versa* as the case now stands.

1st. For the duty of *Chastity* you will not wish me
to undertake any elaborate discussion of its grounds,
nor will it be needful. No one, I presume, will question
that the ideal of a perfect human being is wholly
incompatible with that of licentious relations with the
opposite sex. The perfect human life as conceived
by the cultivated moral consciousness, is essentially
a life of Chastity—not, of course, of *celibacy*, that
is a grievous mistake which we owe to the Christian
Fathers and their violent recalcitration from the
corruption of their epoch—but of real chastity, fidelity
in marriage, or a pure single life. There are indeed
many difficult questions connected with the relations
of the sexes which must be opened up soon when
every old belief is destined to be questioned ; and I fear
there is much trouble and many mistakes and disorders
before us in this direction. But in the end, and after
the needle of the compass has swung backwards and
forwards a little, I am convinced it will point steadily

to the life-long union of one man and one woman, and
to the stern prohibition of unfaithfulness, male or
female. Chief of all I trust will be condemned and
abhorred, that *Venal* Vice which is the opprobrium
of the male sex and the desolation of ours. Let every
woman who is contented to accept the theory that we
are, in a special sense, *made for men*, reflect that here—
in the utter sacrifice, body and soul, of tens of thousands
of women in our land and in all lands,—is the logical
outcome of that vile doctrine. " Women are made for
Men?" Aye! then what matters it if hecatombs of
them are destroyed in a destiny worse than death,
because Men ask for them ? Talk of your Refuges
and your Penitentiaries my well-meaning sisters!
Try them all! You only gather in the wreckage and
driftwood of the relentless tide. Till you lift *Womanhood itself*, you will never arrest, nay you will never
importantly diminish, that dreadful curse, the " great
sin of great cities." Profoundly satisfied am I of this,
—that the cause of the emancipation of women is
identical with that of the purification of society.

I think that women who have never been tempted
to the borders of unchastity, either lured by passion or
driven by the whip of poverty and want, are bound to
speak very gently and pitifully of the falls of their
sisters ; unless they happen to be assured that miserable
vanity and pleasure seeking, and the dry heartless
wickedness we sometimes read of in French novels, of
the class of " *Madame Bovary* " has led them astray.

But I see with some alarm that the growing sense of
the duty of such merciful treatment of the fallen, is
leading not a few in our day to speak as if there was
really no "*fall*" at all,—no change worth mentioning
in a woman's life when she has descended from the
pedestal of her maidenly or wifely purity. It seems
to me that this view is even more dangerous and
further from truth than the too stern and relentless
condemnation of former times. It *is* a vast and almost
immeasurable slip downward from a life of chastity to
one of lawless passion, and the general declension of
the character which usually follows it is a symptom of
how profound is the injury thereby wrought. The sin
can be redeemed, I entirely believe; even the most vice-
enthralled poor wretch, reeling out of a gin palace,
will cast off some time or other in the blessed future,
all pollution as a snake casts its slough. But it is no
mercy to any misguided woman, nor to the community,
to speak as if it were a small matter for the crown of
womanly purity to be cast in the dust.

But my friends, is there no unchastity save that of
the women who bear the brand of adultery or of the
vice stamped as such by society? Surely we must
confess, that there has been many a mercenary, many a
venal marriage, solemnized by a bishop in the most
fashionable churches of London, which has been in
truth nothing else than a deliberate sacrifice of true
chastity,—marriages made without a spark of love
and perhaps endured with disgust for the base sake

of wealth or station? I cannot pursue this painful
subject; but, as I am addressing women to whom the
temptation of a worldly marriage for themselves or
their daughters, is almost the only form in which an
offence against the great duty of Chastity is likely
ever to present itself as a temptation, I must
solemnly record my conviction, that the principle we
all justly accept,—that *Marriage is needful to hallow
Love,* is no whit more true or binding than its
converse, that *Love is needful to hallow Marriage.*

I have just said that worldly marriages are almost
the only temptations of wealthy and well-born
women. But alas, the history of the public scandals
of the last few years reminds me that there is, in some
shameful cases, another. The senseless whirl of amusements in the highest circles seems actually to make
women dizzy, till they fall into the arms of the first
man who catches them. The poor fluttering, foolish
creatures with their heads full of dress and pleasure,
enter the world as if it were a ball-room, and dance
down it, wild with excitement and flattery. Then
suddenly opens under their feet a dark and fathomless
oubliette of shame. We hear a shriek or two, a
murmur of gossip of the bystanders for a little while;
and then they disappear for ever, and the ball-room
sees them no more.

2nd. You will notice that in all this discussion I have
spoken of *Chastity* as a *Personal* Duty and I shall do

exactly the same of *Temperance*. It is true that
Unchastity and Intemperance do harm to the community, and are thus also offences against Social Duty.
But far the worst part of their guilt is its offence
against the man or woman's own soul; the pollution by unchastity of that which was made to be a
temple, or the prostration of the will in brutal intoxication, whereby the power of self-control and self-
direction is lost, and the drunkard sinks below the
level of a hog. Some of you here present will doubtless remember how admirably Channing speaks of this
subject. I do not remember his words, but they were to
this purpose: "Men point to the drunkard's home, his
disordered clothing and maudlin besotted face and
wasted health, and talk as if these constituted the
evils of drunkenness, the reasons why it should be
renounced. But they are only the outward symptoms,
the fitting and rightful symptoms of the dreadful
injury which the man's soul and spirit are undergoing
as he sinks lower day by day abandoning the rank of
a moral and rational being."

It is the fashion just now to say that women are
learning to drink to excess. I believe the same thing
might have been said with as much or greater truth
fifty, or a hundred, or five hundred years ago. As the
proverb has it, "Any stone is good enough to fling at
a dog;" and so some men, and some women also, think
any accusation just which can be levelled at women.
I hope that all who have the progress of women at

heart will refuse to join in this sort of wholesale slander of our sex.*

---

* The loudest in these declamations are the doctors,—men who, if I do not grievously wrong them, have much to answer for in the way of demoralizing weak and impressionable women, in some cases by ordering them stimulants in excessive quantities, and in others by leading them to a deadly concentration of their thoughts upon disorders and weaknesses of their frames of which the less any one thinks the better for mind and body. It is the fashion never to speak of the medical profession without a sickening superfluity of laudatory epithets, which must seem nothing short of ridiculous to the really good and honourable doctors who know very well that (as the *Spectator* remarks) we might just as well praise all the men who pass over Westminster Bridge, as all the variety of characters who obtain medical degrees. For my part I cannot lose this opportunity of addressing my fellow women to say with great seriousness that I believe the old dangers implied in the words "Priests, Women, and Families," were less than the perils of the newer triad, "Doctors, Women, and Families;" and urging every wife and mother to exercise care and vigilance in dealing with a man (if she *will* have a man doctor) who holds to her and her daughters a relation quite as influential as that of the old spiritual director and, if rarely abused, yet assuredly liable to abuse. For one single point I would ask you to reflect upon your experience of that crying grievance and shame of our sex—the valetudinarianism of innumerable fine ladies who, if they were obliged to scrub floors and nurse a dozen children, would probably be ruddy and buxom dames to-morrow; and to consider whether, if their medical attendants did their straightforward duty by them, we should see these women for twenty years on the sofa, their wretched husbands driven from their dispiriting homes, and their children left to governesses and servants, while the doctor draws a comfortable income of fifty or a hundred or two hundred a year from the unhappy household?

That there are now and at all times peculiar temptations for women to intemperance cannot be questioned. The wonder seems to be that with their fluctuating strength and spirits, and all the burdens of suffering and poverty pressing upon the lower classes of women, they yield much more rarely to the *goad* of pain, than men do to the *lure* of the mere pleasure of intoxication. The fact that a drunken woman is so ineffably disgusting a being should not cause us to overlook the palliations which, in the case of the poor, may be offered for her miserable self-abandonment. It is one of the numberless instances of the double harshness wherewith the sins of women are visited, that, till very lately, it has been commonly taken for granted that female drunkards were irreclaimable, and that it was useless to labour for their benefit. I am thankful to hear that there is now in South London a Home for Female Inebriates, which is accomplishing miracles in the way of reformation, under the patronage of that "friend of all the friendless,"—Lord Shaftesbury.

One word of practical caution I will venture to say on this topic to my younger hearers who have not yet tested their own constitutions or powers of self-restraint. Whatever may be the oscillations of your spirits or strength, I entreat of you never to strive to "level them up" by what men now call "nips," but which are, in plain language, "drams." It is these "nips" taken at odd times, or in secret, which create the craving wherein lies the peril. Few people, I believe, become victims of intemperance except through dram-drinking; and it is very doubtful if anybody can persist long in the habit without becoming intemperate. One word more. Let not any doctor or other adviser lead you often to seek relief from pain or sleeplessness in chloral or any other opiate. Be assured that we never play with our brains and nerves without paying sooner or later a heavy penalty in diminished mental power and enfeebled will. These forms of intemperance do not horrify refined women like common intoxication, and do not seem to carry with them the same guilt and degradation; but for that very reason, they are more dangerous; and, as a fact, they partake of the same character and may only too easily lead to similar destruction.

3rd. There is the great Personal Duty of *Veracity*. Again I beg you to note that I classify the obligation to speak Truth as primarily a *Personal* Duty, and only in a secondary sense a *Social* Duty. Truth is, indeed, the *Chastity of the Lips*. Simplicity, Honesty, Veracity of speech and action, are all inevitably included in the conception of a perfect human character. Kant even considers Lying as the worst personal offence, he says, ("*Elementology of Ethics*," Book I, ch. ii), "The highest violation of the duty owed by man to himself, considered as a moral being, singly, is a departure from truth, or lying.

4

That every deliberate untruth in uttering one's thoughts must bear this name in ethics is of itself evident, although in law it be only styled fraud or falsehood, when it violates the rights of others—ethics giving no title to vice on account of its harmlessness; for the dishonour (*i.e.* to be an object of ethical disdain) which it entails accompanies the liar like his shadow. . . . We say nothing here of the damage he may occasion to other people,—the damage being no characteristic of the vice, for it would then be turned into a violation of the duty due to others; nor yet of the damage done by the liar to himself, for then the lie would be a mere error in prudence. . . . A lie is the abandonment, and as it were the annihilation of the dignity of a man."

Starting from this nobler view of the law of Veracity, nothing is more pitiful than to hear the discussions which not unfrequently take place about the lawfulness of saying that which is untrue in one or another contingency. It is of course very easy to imagine these casuistical cases, such as the familiar stock instance of the wife of Hugo Grotius concealing her husband from his enemies, and denying his presence. But as the old Roman, Aulus Gellius, asks pertinently, " If any one says that it is lawful to tell lies on this or that occasion, let us ask him *where* (if we may tell lies at all), he will draw the line and stop? At one lie? or a dozen which may be needful to cover it? Or at sworn lies? Or at a whole series of perjuries?" We may *pardon* a man or woman who in a great and pressing emergency uses a falsehood, just as we may *pardon* a man who amid the roar of cannon loses his nerve and runs away in battle; or a confessor who flinches from the stake. But the true Virtue of Truthfulness knows no exceptions. It is, as I have repeated, a *Personal Duty*, and there is no use in showing that it may be a *social convenience* to neglect it. The personal law of truth cannot be abrogated for any such reason, any more than the personal law of chastity. Most of the disputes and casuistries which have taken place about lies have arisen from the disputants thinking of Truth only as it regarded the *person spoken to*. If they had thought first (as they ought to have done) *of the speaker*, they would have perceived that the facts on which they relied for cancelling the obligations of truth, only touched the *Social* and *Secondary* obligation, and left the *Personal Duty* as fixed as before. If we keep clearly in view that *we are dishonoured* by suffering a Lie to pass our lips (and the better we tell it, the more we are dishonoured), we shall not feel much concern to inquire whether the person to whom we may happen to address our remarks has any right to have truth told *to him*. It is a double sin to tell a Lie to an honest, trustful friend; but it is quite a sufficiently heinous single (*i.e. personal* sin) to tell one to an enemy.

Here again we come on the traces of the miserable heresy of the distinction between masculine and feminine virtue. We are all agreed that a masculine liar ought to be kicked. Why should not a feminine

4 *

liar be sent to Coventry ? I do not know whether the
common accusation be just, and whether women, on the
whole, do tell more falsehoods than men. I am glad
to say I have very few friends who tell lies ! Still, I
think women are not so indignant when their word is
doubted as they ought to be; and that there is a
certain inaccuracy and prevarication common enough
among ladies which we do not find to the same extent
among gentlemen of the same class. When we descend
in the social scale, I am afraid Veracity becomes
more and more rare in either sex, just as it is rare
among all the Southern nations. A clear-sighted friend
once defined to me exactly the sort of shuffling to which
I allude as practised by English ladies, compared to
the frank mendacity of a French woman. Both an
English and a French wife, she supposed, wish to go
to A (some place which their husbands forbade them
to visit). The Frenchwoman goes, and on her return
simply tells her husband she has *not* been to A. The
Englishwoman likewise goes to A, but she also goes
to B, for the express purpose of being able to say she
has gone to B; and on her return she tells her husband
only of her visit to B.

I fear this kind of thing is only too common in some sad
lives—the vice of a servile sex ! God help us out of it.

A good deal of confusion exists, especially in the
minds of some imperfectly educated women, as to the
precise line which separates truthfulness from falsehood,
and nothing is more common than to find in a certain

class what I am always inclined to call the Pharisaism of veracity—the straining at a gnat of small verbal accuracy, while the whole spirit of truthfulness is sometimes absent from the heart. Of this kind is the ridiculous question about saying " Not at Home " to visitors. Of course it would be simpler if we were to adopt the French and Italian form of asking whether a lady " received " that day ; and desire our servants to say that we did, or did not, " receive," as the case might be. But the cordial spirit of English society long ago established the conventional phrase of " Not at Home," as if courteously to imply that, were we in our homes, we should never shut the door on our friends ; and this old-fashioned formula has for a century, I should imagine, been understood by every-body to signify precisely the same as if we said, " Does not receive." What then has the question of Veracity to do with the matter ? Words (it cannot be too often repeated) have no absolute meaning, only the meaning we agree to attach to them, and in which we know they will be understood. If we use words literally exact, but conveying as we know a *false* impression, we incur the guilt of a lie, often of a peculiarly base kind of lie. If, on the contrary, we use a conventional phrase, not exactly or literally describing the fact, but conveying, as we know, a *true* impression, we shall incur no guilt, we have told no lie. I shall return to this subject in discussing the Social Duty of straightfor-wardness with our neighbours.

But is it only in actual speech or written words that we are bound to be truthful ? To me it seems that, for some people, all life is a lie, though they never actually utter a falsehood. Lift your thoughts to what a Truthful Life must be, and see what it includes, and what a noble, splendid thing it would be to live it out ! In such a life there would be nothing to conceal, least of all our convictions on the most solemn topics of human thought. How many thousands of men and women at this particular time keep their opinions on religion a secret, and go on acting as if they believed what they do *not* believe, it would be impossible to calculate. Of course I do not mean to imply that it is any one's duty to make public, or even to speak to their nearest friends, of the vague doubts, the endless weary questionings which torment nearly all thinking minds, at this time of transition. On this point I am much of Gœthe's opinion, " If you have got any Faith, for God's sake give me a share of it ; but you may keep your doubts to yourself ; I have plenty of my own." But when the doubts cease to be merely *gaseous* or fluid, and when they consolidate into crystalized forms of disbelief on one side or belief on the other, then, I think, we are bound to avow the change which has passed over us. It is one of the bad signs of this age that nobody seems willing to bear the smallest inconvenience, or reproach, or coolness from their relatives for the sake of convictions for which our ancestors would have gone to the stocks or the stake.

A man or woman who spends his life with people from whom he carefully conceals the very root and mainspring of his own moral character, is in a position so false, so undignified, so warped and unnatural, that I am at a loss to see how he or she can keep clear of actual mendacity. But even supposing this to be possible, little is gained, for the whole life is mendacious. On the other hand, the advantage to the heart and soul of straightforwardness in this great matter is absolutely measureless. When this is secured, then the "happy warrior" fights evermore under his true colours, and the whole battle of life becomes clear and simplified.

Again, in all our social relations, there is the possibility of being guilty of wretched untruthfulness without actually telling any downright lie. Some miserable people try to appear better born than they are, or to move in better society than they really frequent, and all they say in company is said *avec intention* to convey some impression of their fashion or importance. This seems a childish vanity enough; but it is abominably base and little-minded. And again, women have acquired the shameful reputation of being insincere and treacherous friends, because they falsely make display of the outward tokens of affection towards other women whom they really do not love at all, and whom they ought in candour to treat only with courtesy, not with caresses. All this will come more fully to be considered by-and-bye in speaking of woman's duty in Society.

4th. COURAGE is a Personal Duty. To shrink from pain and danger when we are called on to bear the one or confront the other, is to renounce our moral obligations for a motive so base that even the headlong pursuit of pleasure may be deemed less to attaint the dignity of our nature. The reason why Courage is given its lofty place among masculine virtues is because, like "Great Heart" in "Pilgrim's Progress," it is the guard and protector of the whole company. In the absence of Courage there can be no security against any moral declension whatsoever, since the coward may be bullied and frightened into any crime.

There is no point wherein the great moral heresy of the different nature of Virtue in men and in women has had more miserable consequences than in this matter of Courage; and now we, who renounce that heresy, must make it one of our first cares to develope amongst us this virtue of Courage, hitherto so neglected. We can never be respected by men, can never, indeed, truly respect ourselves, till we are conscious that in the presence of physical danger we shall at least bravely strive to comport ourselves well; and that browbeatings and intimidations will not cause us to budge an inch from the path of duty. Of course no woman can be so dull of observation as not to know that men are invariably flattered by the abject appeal of a woman (especially if she be young and pretty) to save her from some transient peril—a runaway horse—a swaying boat—an irascible bull. Obviously it makes the smallest masculine soul swell with Herculean glory to be clasped round the arms (or in extreme cases, the legs), and beseeched to exhibit the heroism of his sex. Possibly he may be shaking in his shoes, and the application to help anybody but himself may be rather inopportune, especially if the suppliant be plain or elderly. Still, it is rarely resented, and clever women who lay themselves out to charm, are well aware of the fact, and never fail to simulate cowardice even if they happen to possess brazen nerves and too much common sense to apprehend danger where no danger exists. Thus it comes to pass that our sex bears the disgrace, not only of a great deal of genuine poltroonery, but also of much which is mere affectation.

Quite of recent years I am thankful to note many young English ladies are beginning to take pride in physical activity and vigour. They ride across country, take long walking tours, swim, run, play lawn tennis—exhibit, in short, the types of the Dianas, Hippolytas and Atalantas of old. This is a glorious physical reformation which cannot fail to produce far-reaching beneficial consequences on the health and animal spirits both of future women and of the men to whom they will be mothers. Nor will the good results

stop at the invigorated bodily frames, but inevitably
extend to the whole character of women, who will thus
learn to laugh at the affectation of timidity, and take
pride in steady nerves and unflinching "pluck."

Meanwhile, whether you can or cannot share the
benefits of wholesome athletic exercise, there is a
rule which I would earnestly commend to your adoption. Never allow yourselves to talk as if it were
possible for you, when danger comes, to play the
coward. Assume it as a matter of course that you
will always behave bravely, calmly, unselfishly. Then,
when the moment of trial comes, you will, at least,
feel the impulse to do the courageous and heroic thing.
It is possible, of course, that you may flinch; "the
flesh will quiver when the pincers tear," but it will
be against your resolution and intention : involuntary
failure, not a deliberate baseness. If, on the contrary,
you permit yourselves to share the horrid habit (common
now even among young men—more shame to them !)
of proclaiming, with a grin of superior wisdom, that
they never mean to risk their valuable lives for anybody or anything, you will have prepared yourselves to
be dastards, and when the moment arrives, you will
probably show yourselves such, as a matter of course.

It is quite true that in several departments of
Courage it costs us women more effort to be brave
than it costs those iron-nerved, bull-natured men who
are born with the boldness of lions or bull-dogs, and
have all their lives been trained to make courage their

grand point of honour. In place of all this, we have very sensitive frames, and easily-excited nerves; and instead of being trained to make courage our point of honour, we have been caressed and petted in proportion as we have behaved without self command or dignity. But what inference must we draw from these facts ? Simply that we ought to take more pains than men to steady our nerves, to calm our excitement, and to determine resolutely on courageous action wherever we are liable to fail. The virtue which is *innate* with them, must be *acquired* by us. Let us glance over three or four forms of Courage, and observe how women stand as regards them.

First, for the form of passive physical courage which consists in patient endurance of bodily pain as, for example, that of disease, or of a surgical operation. Probably we are here on a par with men in courage, or even before them. The female patients in a hospital, I fancy, will generally be found to complain neither more often nor more loudly than the male patients ; perhaps less so. I once asked a dentist whether gentlemen or ladies gave him most trouble ? and he replied, " O, gentlemen, beyond question. I operated upon a great many officers just before they went to the Crimean war, and I assure you that many of them who are now Balaklava and Inkerman heroes behaved in a very unheroic way indeed in the chair in which you are sitting ! Women scream a little, but are always ready to thank me for what I do for them.

Men moan, and groan, and abuse me!" It would be amusing to inquire whether other dentists make similar reports. Any way, this passive courage is a grand and beautiful virtue. All honour to the women who exhibit it, and make many a sick room seem like a cage where God's bird is practising the songs of Heaven.

Next we have *active* physical courage—the courage which confronts danger and rushes into battle or into fire or water, or amidst the plague-stricken, or which preserves presence of mind amid great accidents, and does calmly and steadily whatever may be possible in self defence or for the defence of others.

This is the order of Courage in which women are specially deficient, but it is instructive to ask further, How and when do they betray the lack of this active physical courage? If I am not mistaken, it will be found that *on great occasions* they are wont to exhibit as much of it as men; and that it is the small insignificant occurrences and accidents wherein they betray themselves so deplorably as cowards. Let us reflect! Were the early Christian women who allowed themselves to be thrown to the lions—or were tortured in a thousand hideous ways—were they dastards? Or the female martyrs in the persecutions of later ages? Or the patriot women, like Judith, or Zenobia, or Boadicea, or Joan of Arc, or Charlotte Corday? To whatever line of heroism men may point, there also we may almost surely find a woman deserving of the

same Cross of Honour. I recollect my father telling me
that in the old Mahratta wars he had scaled the walls
of fortresses while the enemy was hurling stones on
their assailants from the battlements above, and
shooting at them on their ladders from a dozen loop-
holes ; and how at Assaye, he charged with his regiment
(the once famous 19th Light Dragoons), a mere handful
of men, against an almost numberless host, dashing up
again and again to the mouths of the enemy's cannon.
But these things, he said, made little demand on courage.
It was when he and his troop were once ordered to
halt where they had been stationed on a hill-side by
mistake within the *ricochet* of the enemy's balls ; and for
four hours they remained still, while one after another,
the men fell from their horses, cut in twain or left
headless corpses as the shot struck them.   This, he
said, *was* a strain,—such a strain that when the
command to "Charge" was given at last, the roar
wherewith the soldiers responded, revealed the tension
they had undergone.

But courage like this,—or let us say the ever-
memorable noble behaviour of the soldiers on the
sinking "Birkenhead,"—was not greater than was
exhibited by those twenty poor Nuns who, in the
French Revolution, stood together on the scaffold
chanting the *Te Deum*, till one by one the sweet voices
dropped in silence beneath the axe of the guillotine.
Still the survivors sang on with unfaltering lips, till
the Abbess, left alone, gave forth the last "Amen"—and

the glorious Hymn was over. Or, to take another phase of Courage, what man or woman is there who would not have found it easier to ride with the Six Hundred in broad day-light into the Valley of Death at Balaklava, than to have spent a night in the dark in that awful *tête-à-tête* of which we have all lately read, of Sister Dora and the man dying of small-pox ? Even the supreme climax of Courage—that of enduring to see the death rather than the dishonour of those we love, has been attained by a woman. The mother of the seven martyrs, whose story is told in the Books of the Maccabees, may be justly estimated, I think, as the bravest human being on record.

Thus, then, we may be allowed to boast that when *great* demands are made on the physical courage of women, it has not been found lacking. It is before *little* trials, and when there is nothing to call forth the heroism of enthusiasm or. patriotism or religion, that women fail while men preserve their courage. Sir John Bowring once vividly described to me the scene in the wreck of the "Aden" in the Red Sea. He said, he left the crew on deck blaspheming and screaming, mad with terror ; but on going down into the cabin, he found all the ladies on board quietly kneeling round his daughter, who was leading their prayers. Nothing, he added, had ever so forcibly impressed him as an instance of calm courageousness. Yet several of those very women, so nobly brave and self-possessed in the imminent prospect of immediate death, would, I have little doubt, have behaved in quite another way if they had been merely in a pleasure-boat in danger of capsizing in a shallow lake, or in a carriage with a runaway pony, or perhaps in a field with a herd of cows!

Now, as great dangers very seldom knock at our doors and permit us to display our latent heroism, and as small dangers occur every week, I implore my sister women to screw themselves permanently to the sterner pitch; and, like men, make it a rule, once for all, not to "show the white feather" on any occasion, be it little or great.

Lastly, besides passive and active Physical courage, there is Moral courage to be measured. And here again, I believe it will be found that the courage of women *on great occasions* is equal to that of men, but that at ordinary times they are more timid and easily over-crowed and bullied. To dare to speak the truth when it will be turned to our detriment,—to support publicly an unpopular person who is maligned,—to follow conscience through thick and thin in spite of Mrs. Grundy, and probably of a husband who is bound hand and foot to Mrs. Grundy's chariot wheels,—this is a hard lesson; and when we reflect how much heavier are the penalties exacted from women than from men for such independence, we can scarcely wonder that it is more rarely exhibited by our sex. Yet here is undoubtedly a field for the exercise of Courage of greater importance in ordinary and civilized life than any display of physical bravery.

My friends, whenever you hear a silly woman say in
the usual idiotic manner " I am *such* a coward! O
dear, I hope there is no danger ! I am so great
a coward !"—will you please remember henceforth, for
my sake, to ask her, " Good gracious, my dear Madam!
are you also a Liar—or a Thief ? Why should you
confess the one disgrace more than the others ?" And
for yourselves, practise courage, I beseech you, at least
as diligently as you practise the piano. Regard
screaming as a *lèse-majesté* against womanly dignity.
Make it a point of honour to be cool, collected, self
reliant, on all occasions. Do all this only for a few
years, and you will be surprised to find that, after all,
in the small concerns of our smooth English lives,
bravery, like cleanliness, is a cheap virtue. All the
greater the shame when we fail to exhibit it !

Fifthly and lastly, there is a great Personal Duty
of which some of you may never have thought—the duty
of MAINTAINING your own lawful FREEDOM, neither
voluntarily abdicating it, nor suffering it to be wrested
from you. Remember what we have assumed to be the
purpose of life, and consider that the Creator has made
us Moral Free Agents, with all the long train of
mistakes and sufferings and schoolings which that
Freedom involves, for the sake of the great end of
free Virtue ; eternal advance in goodness. Remember that our work in life is to set up His Kingdom,
first within us, and then all round us, in our homes, in

society, and in the world; and then reflect whether
we *dare* permit any human being, whosoever he may
be, to rob us of that Freedom whereby alone that purpose of God in our Creation can be carried out? We
cannot do it, my friends, without incurring almost
suicidal guilt! The obedience of the child—while he *is*
a child, is right and holy, the proper training for the
future self-control of a virtuous life. But there comes
a time when childhood is over, and when the man or
woman enters on the solemn responsibilities of adult life,
and of a Moral Agent made free by God's own decree.
After that hour there is no shifting the responsibility
of our actions, or of our forbearance from action, on
another's shoulders, be that other who he may. Freedom
is the indispensable condition of the whole moral life,
and it follows that the preservation of that Freedom is
one of the first of our Duties. We shall have need
presently to recur to this subject, and estimate the
bearings of the principle now laid down upon many
problems of Social Duty. *Chaste, Temperate, Truthful,
Brave* and *Free*—that is the ideal of PERSONAL VIRTUE
for Woman as for Man.

5

LECTURE III.

Social Duties. Duties of Mothers, Daughters, &c.

I now quit the subject of *Personal Duties,* begging you always to bear in mind that no other obligation can ever come before them; and that in their high practice lies not only our hope of fulfilling the end of our own creation and lifting ourselves nearer to God and goodness, but *also* our best and most unfailing method of blessing and helping our brother men.

I shall for the remainder of this Course treat of the Third great branch of Morals, namely *Social Duties,* and these I shall classify,—not subjectively, as we classified Personal Duties, according to the *virtues to be exercised,* but objectively, according to the *persons to whom Social Duties are owed.*—Such duties, as regards women, will fall into the following groups,—1. The Duties of a Woman as a Member of a Family—Mother, Daughter, Sister, Wife. 2. The Duties of a Woman as Mistress of a Household. 3. As a Member of

Society.   4. As a Citizen of the State and Member
of the Human Race.

Viewing the vast expanse of *Social Duty* before us,
and its ever widening horizon, we may bear with us
two guiding thoughts as general directions to our
efforts.

One thought is, that as *Virtue* is a higher end of
human life than *Happiness,* so whenever we can
conduce to the Virtue of our rational fellow creature,
then that is the proper mode to do our duty by him.
He " that converteth a sinner from the error of his
way," or trains youth to a noble life, does a higher
kind of good than he who nurses the sick or feeds
the hungry.   Second to the helping of our neighbour's
Virtue (we cannot *make* him virtuous, remember!
we can only *conduce* to his virtue), comes the helping
of his Happiness—the relief of his pains and wants,
and the production of his pleasure.   And lastly, there
is a duty owed to those who have still claims on
us, but having no free-will, can have no virtue to
be aided, namely: the lower animals.   For these, all
we can do is, to shield them from pain, and to make
their little lives as pleasurable as we may.   You
will remember Bishop Butler's magnificent statement
of the principle at the root of all social morality;
— that it *is on the simple fact of any creature
being sentient, i.e.,* capable of pain and pleasure,—on
which is founded our obligation to save it pain and
afford it pleasure.

5 *

Again, we may take with us through all the range
of duty this other guiding thought,—that in doing
our duty we are fulfilling the blessed task of establish-
ing "*God's Kingdom*," the Kingdom of Justice, Truth,
and Love. Our *Personal* Duty is the setting up of a
little Divine Kingdom in our own breasts; our *Social*
Duty is the extending of that Kingdom; first making
our homes a *province* of it; then spreading it as best
we may and as our poor powers may permit, in all
directions, looking forward to the time, far off
perhaps down the ages, but still drawing nearer, when
"the earth shall be full of the knowledge of the Lord
as the waters cover the seas," and when (as the Parsees
say every morning in their prayers) "Ormuzd shall
conquer, and Ahrimanes be subdued and converted,
and Hell be abolished, and love and joy reign for
ever."

> " The one far-off divine Event
> Towards which the whole creation moves."

Now we labour towards that blessed end, often in
darkness and sorrow; but out of the cloud there comes
to cheer us many a ray of hope, if we be of those,—

> " Who rowing hard against the stream
> See distant gates of Eden gleam,
> And do not dream it is a dream."

I confess I love this thought of working for the
"Kingdom of God," and find it infinitely cheering and
comforting. We are beset and harassed in these days

with doubts of every sort. But this idea of a Divine
Kingdom comes home to us all! Even if we have
been so unhappy, so infinitely unhappy, as to lose
sight for a time, behind the clouds which veil His
Throne, of the *King* Himself, we can still labour to
promote what we meant of old by " His *Kingdom*. We
may join hand in hand, all of us who are working for
any kind or sort of good—to relieve Want or Pain ;
to teach Truth; to stop Cruelty ; to obtain Freedom;
to bestow innocent happiness—each and all we may
recognize each other and ourselves as fellow labourers
in God's vineyard; servants and soldiers of the same
Kingdom. And whether we are able in words to pray
together or not, we may feel that we are all *living the
Prayer*, " Thy Kingdom Come"—the central clause of
the world's great prayer—which we effectually offer
whenever from our hearts we desire to see JUSTICE
done and TRUTH prevail, and LOVE be Lord of all.

To clear the ground for the solution of several
difficult problems of social duty which will, by-and-bye,
come before us, we must begin by defining, as
accurately as may be, the nature and order of Social
Duties. The Canon already quoted, " Love thy neighbour as Thyself," gives us the *spirit* of the whole.
For more accurate ethical terminology, it will be
useful to take the word " Benevolence" (the best trans-
lation in this context of the Pauline "ἀγάπη"), and make
it the corner stone of our edifice. We may say, " We

owe Benevolence to all our fellow-creatures," and use this as a fundamental Axiom or Canon, from which all that is to follow may be deduced.

The old Schoolmen very properly distinguished between Love of *Complacency,* (or what we should call *Affection*), and Love of *Benevolence.* The former, from the nature of things, must be free and spontaneous, and it can be no *duty* to feel it towards any one. The latter alone, the Love of Benevolence, is a sentiment *owing* to all mankind, and which we can and ought to feel to every creature. This is a very deep and important ethical distinction to which I shall often have occasion to refer. I must remark, however, that whenever Love of Benevolence rises to its true pitch, and becomes the Enthusiasm of Humanity or heartfelt Altruism, it has a blessed tendency to get transformed into Love of Complacency. If it be surely true (in spite of Mr. Darwin) that "we hate those whom we have injured," it is happily at least equally true that we love those whom we have benefited, or wished to benefit, with something exceedingly like Affection.*

---

* To those amongst us who have not bowed to the new moral system of Darwin and Spencer, there is something almost pathetic in the ignorance both of the passions and also of the spiritual part of human nature which these philosophers unconsciously betray. Mr. Darwin, engaged in an inquiry concerning that very curious thing, Repentance, and the question, "Why does man regret that he has followed one natural impulse rather than another, and why does he feel that he ought to regret his conduct?"—arrives at the conclusion

Benevolence, then, is to be accepted as the universal principle of Social duty, and to be understood in the

that the selfish passions, once gratified, always fade, and the social ones resume their influence. "Thus, as man cannot prevent old impressions from passing through his mind, he will be compelled to compare the weaker impressions of, for instance, past hunger, or of vengeance satisfied with the instinct of sympathy and goodwill to his fellows, which is still present and ever in some degree active in his mind;"—and so he will feel dissatisfied with himself. ("*Descent of Man*," p. 90.) Surely (as in reviewing this book at the time of its appearance, I ventured to remark), "the reader might be excused who should figure to himself the author as a man who has never in his life-time had cause seriously to repent a single unkindly or ignoble deed, and who has unconsciously attributed his own generous and placable nature to the rest of his species, and proceeded to argue as if the world were made of Darwins?" Where, we ask in bewilderment, where are the people to be found in whom "sympathy and goodwill" to all their neighbours exist in the state of permanent instincts, whose resentful feelings die out as a matter of course after every ebullition and leave them in perfect charity with their neighbours, not as the *result* of repentance, but as its *preliminary?* In what Island of the Blessed may we find the men and women for whom the precept "Love your enemies" is a mere platitude,—and Tacitus' remark a calumny that " *Humani generis proprium est odisse quem læseris?*" (It is natural to human beings to hate those whom we have injured.)

This whole system of Morals wherein the two greatest forces at work in man's life seem equally ignored,—the enormous brute force of the physical and irascible passions on one side, and the power of Divine Spiritual might on the other—the Flesh which lusts against the Spirit and the Spirit which lusts against the flesh—has been well summed up by one of its latest and most clear-headed disciples, M. ALFRED FOUILLÉE, in the *Revue des Deux Mondes.* I beg to extract the

double sense of an *inward* genuine good will, and of
a practical readiness to carry out that good will in
beneficent *action*. I hope it is needless to dwell on these
last points. There are, indeed, people who imagine
they do all they are required when they *give* this or
that, or *do* something or other for their neighbour.
Nay! but I hold that nobody has a right,—that it is
an insolence and a presumption,—to give or do anything for our fellow man unless we entertain in our
hearts a genuine wish to serve him. If we do anything of the kind from any other motive, from osten-

following passage from his brilliant articles, as touching to
my mind the very Nadir of Morals, and embodying as nearly
as possible all that I think to be most false, debasing and
perilous in the speculations of this, now paramount, school.

"On le voit la doctrine de l'évolution telle que l'entendent
MM. Darwin et Spencer, remplace l'obligation morale du
spiritualisme par une sorte d'obligation physique ou de nécessité
naturelle qui entraine l'individu d'abord à son bien propre, puis
au bien commun. . . Il faut montrer (et c'est ce qu'a essayé
M. Spencer) par quelle évolution inévitable des êtres dont
chacun cherche son propre bonheur, finiront par chercher
nécessairement le bonheur de tous. Pour obtenir ce résultat,
c'est moins aux préceptes abstraits qu'il faut faire appel qu'à
l'entrainement de l'education, à la puissance des lois publiques,
surtout à l'action lente de l'heredité et de la sélection naturelle;
car ce n'est pas une moralité métaphysique qu'il s'agit de pro-
duire chez les hommes, c'est 'une moralité organique,' et
en quelque sorte physique, qui sera présente aux organes et
inhérente à la constitution même du cerveau humaine comme
la douceur est devenu inhérente aux animaux apprivoisés."—
"La Moralité Contemporaine," par Alfred Fouillée.—*Revue des
Deux Mondes*, July 1880, p. 123.

tation, or as a hard piece of justice, or for the purpose
of self-training and discipline, we are absolutely *in-
sulting* our brother.

I remember once in visiting that awful place, the
hospital *degli Incurabili* at Rome, in the Via dei Greci,
being implored by scores of wretched dying creatures
to give them money to buy coffee and other things
which might in some degree have assuaged their
misery, but which the hospital could not provide. As
one ghastly figure after another sat up in bed as I
passed down the vast ward, and exposed with ve-
hement gestures and cries for pity the dreadful sores
and cancers of which each was perishing, I felt like
Dante passing through one of the *giri* of hell. Naturally I turned to the placid nun who accompanied me,
and asked, " Were there no Italian lady-visitors to the
Hospital ?" " Yes, there were very many saintly ladies
the Contessa So-and-so, the Principessa So-and-so."
" And do they not give what they want to these poor
souls?" " No, they do not come for that purpose." " In
heaven's name what *do* they come for, then ?" " *Per
pettinarle*, Signora." It was some time before I could
be made to understand. These fine ladies came to
mortify *themselves* by performing the disgusting office
of combing the dishevelled and filthy hair of the
hapless creatures ! Of the idea of affording them
such relief as their sufferings might receive, they were
wholly innocent.

No, my friends : We must not " *make our salva-*

tion" in the next world, or make our reputation in this, out of our fellow creatures needs and our largesses and services. That will never do. We must *begin* with the sympathy; and then, and then only, feel at liberty to perform the divine and blessed task of helping our brother.

Secondly, there comes the practical Action of beneficence; and here our subject naturally ramifies under the different heads under which I have classed these Addresses. Benevolence, true Charity, must indeed "begin at home." On the universal law of Benevolence we must place the natural *rider*—that we owe Benevolence *first*, a *precedency*, of all its manifestations, to those *nearest* to us; and that their claims must be satisfied (so far as may be) prior to the extension of our efforts to satisfy those further off. This precedency of claims must of course follow the circumstances of life.

First, there is the supreme priority founded on the natural ties of *proximity in blood*; the reciprocal first claims of Parents and Children, and then of Brothers, and so on. The fulfilment of these claims constitutes *Parental, Filial* and *Fraternal Duty.*

Second, there is precedency founded on *Contract*,—the mutual claims of Husbands and Wives, founded on the great formal contract of Marriage; and the claims of Friends, founded on an informal, but, in some cases, scarcely less morally sacred, tacit contract. The fulfilment of these claims constitutes *Conjugal* and *Friendly Fidelity.*

Thirdly, there is the precedency founded on the claim of *prior indebtedness ;* the individual having already exhibited Benevolence towards us and having a just right to expect the same in return. The fulfilment of this claim is *Gratitude.*

Lastly, there are the remoter claims of *local Propinquity,* by which the dwellers under our roof, our immediate neighbours, and our countrymen, have a certain right to expect that we shall not pass over them to attend to the (similar) wants of remoter persons and nations.

We begin to-day with the special claims to Benevolence founded on the *natural ties of blood,*—and first with the reciprocal claims of Parents and Children.

There is to many of us something painful and harsh in attempting to define as stern *duties* the conduct and feelings which spring spontaneously from our hearts. Most of us are happy enough to feel, or to have felt, that we needed no law to command us to do all that in us lay, to sacrifice health or wealth or anything we possessed, for a beloved parent or an idolized child. Love has been to us *the* fulfilling of the Law, and the law consequently became superfluous, making it seem almost an impertinence to refer to it. This is surely the natural state of things. It does not generally need (happily for us) any transcendent virtue on the part of the parent to make the child love it, nor any special gifts or graces on the part of the child to make the parent cherish it. It is "Nature's law divine" that those she has so closely united "cannot choose but love." Each sacrifices to each without moral effort, in the pure spontaneity of complete affection, the aim of the other's welfare the only rule, and the idea of having promoted it the only possible reward.

Let those among you who are too young to know all that family affection means (and nobody *can* know it till they are able to compare it with other social sentiments) take my word for this, that nothing is ever like it, nothing will ever take its place. When the last duty of filial love is paid, and there remains nothing more for us to do for the beloved one for ever —when the form we cherished and sheltered from every breath lies out away in its lonely grave, round which the snow is falling and the winter winds are raving—then it seems as if all other duties are in comparison so remote, so indifferent, so devoid of all sacredness, that it is hard to rouse ourselves to fulfil them, save by the thought "My Father,—or my Mother,— would have wished it." And again, on the other side, the Parental love which fills a woman's heart when she holds her little child in her arms is (as even we childless ones must see) something so divine, so pure from all selfishness where it is felt aright, that every care and fatigue and sacrifice comes to the mother as a matter of course. Even the brutes show this. The cat will burn herself to save her kittens from the flames—

the timid bird confronts danger and even invites the cruel sportsman to follow her that he may leave her nest undisturbed.

Our task, however, is not to dilate on parental and filial affection, but to define the underlying lines of *duty* which, when the affection is unhappily defective or misguided, must afford to both parent and child the permanent rule of conduct.

Referring to the canon of Social Duty, we find that the claim of children on parents and *vice versa* is a *supreme claim to Benevolence*, that is, each is bound to seek the other's welfare before all other objects, or in other words to endeavour to conduce to their virtue and to produce their happiness.

For reasons which will hereafter appear, we shall discuss first the Duties of Parents.

A conscientious Mother, aiming before all things at the moral good of her child, and feeling the tremendous responsibilities which rest on her as regards all its future life for weal or woe, must, I should think, often be nearly overwhelmed with her task. Poor Margaret Fuller, recording in her diary the event of her child's birth, must have expressed the thoughts of thousands : " I am the Mother of an immortal being ! God be merciful to me, a sinner !" The sense of her own unworthiness and incapacity for her sacred task was probably, however, the very best preparation for performing it well. The woman who thinks herself quite equal to the duties of Motherhood, almost

betrays by that fact that she has only the meanest
notions of their nature and extent.

I hope you, my friends, who are Mothers, and possess
the experience which I shall never know, will pardon
my presumption in laying down before you what
appears to me the leading outlines of parental duty.
If these could be generally agreed upon, the correlative
duties of children, about which so much doubt and
friction at present prevail, would become more clear.

Let me say something very serious to you at this
point, something which I think we ought to bear in
mind, not only in considering parental, but all other
social duties. We often refer to the Love of God as
the supreme love, and most justly, for all the holy love
which ever swelled in a mother's breast can only have
come from Him,—a drop from the Fountain,—a ray
from the Sun. But have you ever reflected that in
that awful Love of God for His poor children of clay,
there must be mingled at once infinite tenderness and
pity, and at the same time a severity which never
shrinks from any suffering needed to recall us from sin,
or purify, or sanctify us? That is the Ideal of all Love—
the *norm* towards which we should strive to lift our
poor, feeble, short-sighted, selfish affections ; and which
it above all concerns a parent to strive to translate
into the language of human duty. This is the truest
love, the love which attaches itself to the very soul of the
child, which *repents with it*, with tears bitterer than its
own, for its faults, and, while heaping on it so far as

may be every innocent pleasure, never for an instant abandons the thought of its highest and ultimate welfare. I think that till a parent's love for a child is of the *same character* with that Divine Love of which we learn somewhat in life's supremest hours of communion,—till then his, or her, love is poor and faulty.

But O, what a wondrous, what a sublime thing it is for a Mother to be able to feel towards her offspring something like what God feels to us all! Kepler said one of the grandest things ever uttered when he discovered the law of the planetary distances, and bowed his head and said in awe-struck tones, "O God! I think Thy thoughts after Thee." We do, effectually, "think God's thoughts" whenever we study Nature. But it is higher still (if I may dare to use the words) to *feel God's feelings,*—to love even one little child as He loves it. And such divine sort of motherly love has this exceeding glory, that all through life it will remain as the token, the assurance to the child, that there *is such a thing as Perfect Love in the Universe.* He has felt it, he has been cradled in its arms, he has learned to trust it absolutely, and to know that however often or however miserably he may fail, that Love will never forsake him, but will lift him up and restore him at last.

A Mother's love, then, ought to be attuned to the very note of the Love Divine,—to be in fact its echo from the deep cave of her heart.

But with such super-earthly love to light her way, what does she see before her ? There is, first, the duty of conducing to her child's Moral welfare,—the highest of all her duties ; secondly, of securing his bodily health ; thirdly, of giving him that intellectual training which will enlarge his being and make his moral nature itself more robust and capable of fulfilling his duties in life ; and lastly, of making him as happy as she may. These are each and all most complicated problems to many a good mother, working perhaps against wind and tide, with feeble health, or limited means ; or possibly with a husband who thwarts and opposes her endeavours. It would require not half a lecture but a whole treatise to deal with such a subject fitly, even if I possessed the experience or insight needful for the task. There is only one point on which I think ethical science may be of some utility. That point is the problem of *obedience.* How far ought it to be enforced ?

Three things are commonly confounded in speaking of Filial Obedience.

1st. The obedience which must be exacted from a child for its own physical, intellectual, and moral welfare.

2nd. The obedience which the parent may exact for his (the parent's) welfare or convenience.

3rd. The obedience which parent and child alike owe to the Moral Law and which it is the parent's duty to teach the child to pay.

If Mothers would but keep these three kinds of obedience clear and distinct in their minds, I think much of the supposed difficulty of the problem would disappear. And if children as they grow up would likewise discriminate between them, many of their troubles would be relieved.

For the first, the excellent old Dr. Thomas Brown lays down (*"Lectures on Ethics,"* p. 287) a principle which seems to me exactly to fit the case. He says that parents "should impose no restraint *which has not for its object some good greater than the temporary evil of the restraint itself."* For an infant the restraint is no evil, and at his age everything *must* be a matter of obedience, the babe possessing no sense or experience for self-guidance. But as childhood advances so should freedom advance ; and even if the little boy oɩ girl do now and then learn by sharp experience, the lesson will generally be well worth the cost ; whereas the evils of over restraint have no compensation. Each one is bad in itself, checking the proper development of character, chilling the spirits, and also in a cumulative way becoming increasingly mischievous as the miserable sense of being fettered becomes confirmed.

In all this matter of the child's own welfare, the Mother's aim ought to be to become the lifelong *Counsellor* of her child ; and a Counsellor is (by the very hypothesis) one who does not persist in claiming *authority*. Nobody thinks of *consulting* another who may conclude their "advice" by saying "And now I *order* you to do as I have advised." To drop, as completely and as early as possible the tone of command, and assume that of the loving, sympathetic, ever-disinterested Guide and Friend—that is, I think, the true wisdom of every Mother, as it was that of my own. Of course there are cases so grave (especially where girls, who little understand the need of caution, are concerned), that it is absolutely necessary, nay, the mother's pressing duty, to prohibit her daughter from running into danger. To apply Brown's rule, the evil of the restraint is more than counterbalanced by immunity from deadly peril. Perhaps it is one of the principal causes of the dissatisfaction of young girls with parental control that they do not, and cannot, understand the horrible dangers which may overtake them in the still foul condition of society.

2nd. It is too little remembered that a parent has a moral right to exact obedience as a form of *service* from his child. The parent has, in strictest ethical sense, the first of all claims on the child's *special benevolence, i.e.* on his *will to do good.* The double ties of Gratitude and of closest human Relationship, make it the duty of the child to pay that sacred debt from first to last; and it is entirely fit and greatly for its benefit that the parent should claim that duty. The parent's *direction* in such cases, properly translated, is not a *Command,* to which the response is blind obedience; but an *indication of the way in which the person to*

whom the debt is due, desires that it should be paid.
There ought to be nothing in the slightest degree
harsh or dictatorial in such direction.   On the contrary,
I cannot but think that the introduction by parents of
much greater courtesy to their children would be an
immense advantage in this and other cases.   We all
ask our servants politely to do for us the services which
they have contracted to do, and for which we pay them.
How much more kindly and courteously ought we to
ask of our children to perform services due by the
blessed and holy debt of nature and gratitude, and which
ought, each one, to be a joy to the child as well as to
the parent!   When it is rightly demanded and cheerfully paid, how excellent and beautiful to both is this
kind of filial duty!   When, for example, we see little
girls of the working classes taught to carry their father's
dinner to the field as soon as they can toddle, and
helping their mother to " mind the baby," even if it
be a " little Moloch " of a baby,—we witness both the
fulfilment of a legitimate claim on the part of the parents,
and a most beneficent moral training for the child.   I
think this sort of *service* of the child is sadly lacking
among the richer classes, and that it would be an excellent thing if mothers, however wealthy, found means
of making their children more useful to themselves.
Nothing can be worse for a child than to find everything
done for her, and never to be called upon to do anything
for anybody else. Indeed any fine-natured child, like a
dog, will find much more real pleasure in being of use—

6 *

or fancying it is so—than in being perpetually pampered and amused. Of course there would be moral limits to such claims on the parents' part, as, *e.g.*, when they would interfere with the child's health or education. But there is no natural termination in point of age to the parent's right to give such directions for his own service. On the contrary, the time when the adult son or daughter has come into the full possession of his or her faculties, while the parent is sinking into the infirmities of age, is the very time when Filial Duty is most imperative in its obligation ; and the fact that aged parents rarely attempt to give to adult sons and daughters the same directions for their comfort as they gave them when children, shows how little the real nature of these sacred rights and duties is commonly understood.

3rd. There is the *Obedience* which both parent and child owe *to the eternal Moral Law ;* and this obedience again ought to be kept perfectly distinct from that which is exacted either for the child's personal welfare or the parent's convenience. The old and most important distinction between a thing which is *malum in se* and a thing which is only *malum prohibitum,* ought never to be lost sight of. Even in a very little child, I think, a moral fault, such as a lie, or cruelty to an animal, or vindictiveness towards its companions, ought to be treated with gravity and sadness ; and as the child grows, an importance ought to be attached to such faults wholly incommensurate

with any other sort of error, such as indolence about
lessons or the like. The one aim of the parent must
be to make a profound impression of the awfulness and
solemnity of moral good and moral evil.

But even here the difficulty haunts us: When is
this enforcement of obedience to moral laws to cease?
So long as a child is absolutely compelled to do right
by sheer force and terror of punishment, its moral
freedom can have no scope, and its moral life consequently cannot even begin. It cannot acquire the
virtue which results from free choice. All that the
parent can do (and it is an indispensable preparation for virtue, though not virtue itself) is first to
teach the child what is right—to draw out its latent
moral sense, and inspire it with the wish to do right—
and then to *help its steps* in the path which has been
pointed out. Once a child grasps the idea of Duty, and
begins in its little way to try and " be good," and
displays the indescribably touching phenomena of
childlike penitence and restoration, it becomes surely
the most sacred task for the mother to aid such efforts—
silently indeed for the most part, and too reverentially to
talk much about it—with tenderest sympathy. It would
be no kindness, of course, but cruelty to open up hastily
ways of liberty before moral strength has been gained
to walk in them. The " hedging up the way with
thorns " is a Divine precaution which a mother may well
imitate. But the *principle* must be, as in the case of
directions in matters not moral, gradually and system-

atically to exchange directions and orders for counsels and exhortations.

And here, in closing these, perhaps, too tedious remarks on the moral training of children, I shall add a word which may possibly startle some who hear me, —Beware that in earnestly seeking your child's moral welfare, you do not *force* the moral nature with hot-house culture. To be a sturdy plant it must grow naturally and not too rapidly. It seems as if it were not intended by Providence that this supreme part of our human nature should be developed far in childhood and early youth, lovely as are the blossoms it some-times then bears,—too often to drop into an untimely grave, or wither away in the heat of manhood without fruit. Dr. Arnold of Rugby undoubtedly made a great mistake in this matter, as one of his very best disciples, Arthur Hugh Clough, was able in later years to see. Mothers should not be unhappy,—their boys being honourable, and affectionate,—if they should, at fifteen, prefer a game of football to a visit of charity; and I should not blame at all severely any of my young friends (if such there be here present) who may be at this moment wishing that she were playing lawn-tennis, instead of sitting still to hear a dull dissertation on moral philosophy !

But when all is done that can be done by human wisdom to help the moral growth of the young, there is a vast space left for the other and easier parental duty of *Providing for their Happiness*. Of course to

nine parents out of ten, high and low, it is the joy and
delight of their lives to make their children as happy
as possible.   There is no virtue in this.   Nature (or
let us say frankly, God) has so made us that in middle
life nearly all direct pleasures, to be enjoyed on our
own account, begin to pall.   We are too busy or too
indifferent to care much for a score of things which,
when we were younger, we found quite entrancing.

"It is the one great grief of life to feel all feelings die."

But just as our sun goes down to the horizon,
a moonlight reflection of pleasure, purer, calmer than
the first, rises to give a sweet interest to the lives
of all who are happy enough to have young creatures
around them.   The pleasures we can no longer taste
for ourselves, we taste in our children's enjoyment.
Their glee, their eagerness, their freshness of delight,
stir our pulses with tenderness and sympathy.   I do
not know anything in the world which pulls one's
heartstrings so much as the sight of a little blue-
eyed, golden-haired, white-frocked atom of humanity,
clapping its hands and crowing with ecstasy at the
sight of a kite soaring up into the summer sky.

Are we to ask parents to deny themselves and their
children in the stern old way, and turn their young
lives into dreary rounds of duty and work, till they
hate the very name of either one or the other ?   God
forbid !   Does GOD, the great Parent, Father and
Mother of the World, lead us up to Himself by any

such harsh and stern tuition ?   Nay, but has He not
made earth so beautiful, and planted flowers by
every wayside, and gladdened our hearts by ten
thousand delights of the intellect, the senses, the
tastes and the affections ?   Fear, my friends, to make
your children *unhappy,* and to love them *too little.*
But never fear to make them too happy or to love
them too much !   There is a great deep saying, that
we must all enter the Kingdom of God as little
children.   Surely the converse of it is true also, and
we should prepare in our homes a Kingdom of God,—of
peace and love and tenderness and innocent pleasure,
—whenever a little child is sent to us out of heaven to
dwell in it ?

We now come to speak of the DUTIES OF DAUGHTERS.
The ethical grounds of the duty of supreme Benevolence towards our Parents are clear.   They are
nearest to us of human beings ; we owe them life, and
(nearly always also) endless cares and affection.   In the
case of a Mother, her claims on her child—founded on
the bodily agony she has borne on its behalf, and the
ineffably sweet office of nursing, (when she has
performed it) ; her care in infancy and love and
sympathy in later years,—make together such a
cumulative title to gratitude and devotion that it is
impossible to place on it any limitation.

This claim is, of course, happily usually admitted in
the case of Daughters *who do not marry.*   It is under-

stood that they are bound to do all they can for their mother's and father's comfort. But may I ask, *who* absolved the daughters *who marry* from the same sacred obligation? In Catholic countries young women often quit their aged parents, no matter how much they need them, to "enter religion," as it is said, and we Protestants are very indignant with them for so doing. But when it comes to our Protestant religion of Matrimony, lo! we are extremely indulgent to the girl who deposits her filial obligations on what the *Morning Post* calls the "Hymeneal Altar!" The daughter practically says to her blind father or bedridden mother, " Corban! I am going off to India with Captain Algernon, who waltzes beautifully, and who I met last night at a ball. It is a gift, by what-soever you might have been profited by me."

Is this right or justifiable? Public opinion condones it, and the parent often consents out of the abundance of unselfish affection, thereby in a certain formal way releasing the daughter from her natural debt. But I do not think, if the parent really *wants* her services, that she can morally withdraw them, even with such consent, and certainly not without it.

We all see this remarkably clearly when the question is not of Marriage, but a girl of the higher class de-voting herself to Charity, or Art, or any kind of public work which requires her to quit her parents' roof. Then, indeed, even if her parents be in the full vigour of life, and have half-a-dozen other daughters, we are pretty sure to hear the solemn condemnation of the adventurous damsel; "Angelina ought to attend to her father and mother, and not go,—here or there,—for this or that purpose."

Surely there is a very obvious rule to cover all these cases? If either parent *wants* the daughter, she ought not to leave him or her, *either* to marry or to go into a nunnery or for any other purpose. If her parents do *not* want her, then, being of age to judge for herself, she is free *either* to undertake the duties of a wife, or *any others* for which she may feel a vocation?

This may sound very hard. It is undoubtedly the demand for a very high degree of *virtue* where the sacrifice may be that of the happiness of a lifetime. But *every* duty may sometimes claim such sacrifices. Parental duty does so perpetually. How many thousands of mothers and fathers toil all their days and give up health and every enjoyment for their children's interests. Why should not Filial duties likewise exact equal sacrifice? The *entire* devotion to the parent when the parent really needs it, and the constant devotion of *as much* care as the parent requires— this, and nothing short of this, seems to me to be the standard of Filial Duty.

A hard problem is presented by the case of the abnormal and scarcely sane development of selfishness which we sometimes sadly witness in old age. I think in such deplorable cases the child is called on to remember

that, even in her filial relation, the *moral welfare* of the
object of Benevolence is before all other considerations,
and that she is bound to pause in a course which
obviously is tending to promote a great moral fault.
Gently and with great care and deference she ought
to remind the parent of the needs of others.

The great difficulty in the lives of hundreds of
daughters of the upper ranks just now lies in this :
that they find themselves torn between two opposing
impulses, and know not which they ought to follow.
On one side are the habits of a child, and the assurance of everybody that the same habits of quiescence
and submission ought to be maintained into womanhood. On the other hand there is the same instinct
which we see in a baby's limbs to stir, to change its
position, to climb, to run, to use in short the muscles
and faculties it possesses. Every young bird flutters
away from its nest, however soft ; every little rabbit
quits the comfortable hole in which it was born ; and
we take it as fit and right they should do so, even
when there are hawks and weasels all around. Only
when a young girl wants to do anything of the
analogous kind her instinct is treated as a sort of sin.
She is asked : " Cannot she be contented, having so nice
a home and luxuries provided in abundance ?" Keble's
fine, but much misused, lines about " Room to deny
ourselves," and the " common task " and " daily
round " being all we ought to require, are sure to be
quoted against her ; and in short she feels herself a

culprit, and probably at least once a week has a fit of
penitence for her incorrigible "discontent." I have
known this kind of thing go on for years, and
it is repeated in hundreds, and thousands of families.
I have known it where there were seven miserable big
young women in one little house! It is supposed to
be the most impossible thing in the world for a parent
to give his son a stone for bread, or a serpent for a fish.
But scores of fathers, in the higher ranks, give their
daughters diamonds when they crave for education;
and twist round their necks the serpents of idle
luxury and pleasure when they ask for wholesome
employment.

Pardon me if I speak very warmly on this subject,
because I think here lies one of the great evils of
the condition of our sex and class at this time; and
I feel intensely for the young spirits whose natural and
whose *noble* aspirations are so checked and deadened and
quenched through all their youth and years of energy,
that, when the time for emancipation comes at last, it
is too late for them to make use of it. They have been
dwarfed and stunted, and can never either be, or do,
anything greatly good.

In short, the complaint we women make against men,
that they persist in treating us as Minors when we
have attained our Majority, is what daughters too
often can justly make against both their fathers and
mothers. They keep them in the swaddling clothes of
childhood when they ought to set free and train

every limb to its most athletic and joyous exercise.
Dangers, of course, on the other side there are, of over-
emancipated and ill-advised girls who sorely need more
parental guidance than they obtain ; but so far as my
experience goes, these cases are few compared to those
of the young women (ladies, of course, I mean, for in
the lower classes such evils are unknown) whose
lives are spoiled by *over-restraint in innocent things.*
They are left free and encouraged to plunge into the
Maëlstrom of a London Season's senseless whirl of
dissipation and luxury. They are restrained from
every effort at self-development or rational self-sacrifice, till, for the very want of some corrective bitter,
they go and beat the hassocks in an Eaton Square
church as a pious exercise, or perhaps finally lock
themselves up in Clewer or East Grinstead. Small
blame to them ! Ritualist Nunneries at present offer
the most easily accessible back-door out of Belgravian
drawing-rooms into anything like a field of usefulness.

Now for SISTERS. That Brothers and Sisters should
give one another in an ordinary way the first fruits
of their Benevolence, follows obviously from the
closeness of their *Propinquity.* Usually there has also
been from childhood the blessed interchange of kind-
nesses which accumulate on both sides into a claim
of reciprocal *Gratitude.*

Miss Bremer remarks that, " It is the general

characteristic of affection to make us blind to faults
of those we love, but from this weakness *fraternal*
love is wholly exempt!" Brothers are indeed terrible
critics of their sisters, and so far irritating creatures.
But otherwise, as we all know, they are the very joy
and pride of our lives; and there is probably not one
duty in our list which needs less to be insisted on to
women generally than that of bestowing on their
brothers not only Love of Benevolence, but also a
large amount of Love of Complacency. It is usually
also a truly sound *moral* sentiment; causing the Sister
to take profound interest in the religious and moral
welfare of her brother, as well as in his health and
happiness.

One mistake, I think, is often made by sisters, and
still more often by mothers, to which attention should
be called. The unselfishness of the sisters and the
fondness of the mother for her boy, and the fact that
the boy is but rarely at home, all contribute to a habit
of sacrificing everything to the young lad's pleasure
or profit, which has the worst effect on his character
in after life. Boys receive from women themselves in
the nursery, and when they come home from school
in the holidays, a regular *education in selfishness.*
They acquire the practice of looking on girls and
women as persons whose interests, education and
pleasures must always, as a matter of course, be postponed to their own. In later life we rue—and their
wives may rue—the consequences!

The duties of Sisters to Sisters are even more close and tender than those of Sisters to Brothers. I hardly know if there be any salient fault in the usual behaviour of English Sisters to one another which any moral system could set right. Perhaps the one quality oftenest deficient in this, and other more distant family relationships,—to which we need not further refer— (Uncles, Aunts, Cousins, and so on), is *courtesy*. " Too much familiarity," as the proverb says, " breeds contempt." The habit of treating one another without the little forms in use among other friends, and the horrid trick of speaking rudely of each other's defects or mishaps, is the underlying source of half the alienation of relatives. If we are bound to show *special benevolence* to those nearest to us, why on earth do we give them pain at every turn, rub them the wrong way, and *froisser* their natural *amour propre* by unflattering remarks or unkind references ? For once we can do them a real service of any kind, we can (if we live with them) hurt, or else please, them fifty times a-day. The individual who thinks she performs her duty to daughter or sister, or niece, while she waits to do the exceptional services, and hourly frets and worries and humiliates her—is certainly exceedingly mistaken. The genuine *benevolence*—the *" will to make happy"*—will take a very different course.

It will not be necessary here to pursue further the

subject of the Duties arising from the ties of Natural Relationship. Holy and blessed things that they are! I am persuaded that even the best and happiest of us only half apprehend their beautiful meaning, and that we must look to the life beyond the grave to interpret for us all their significance.

In the next Lecture we shall discuss a very difficult question indeed—the Duties of a Wife—and then the Duties of the Mistress of a Household.

LECTURE IV.

Duties of Contract—Wives—Friends.

PASSING from Duties arising from the ties of *Blood-Relationship* (Parents and Children, Sisters, Brothers and so on), we reach the exceedingly important class of Duties founded on *Contract;* pre-eminently on the great Contract of MARRIAGE.

The formal Marriage Contract of most civilized nations includes two *natural,* and one *artificial* obligation.

First there is the mutual promise of Conjugal Union, to which is added a mutual engagement of exclusive Fidelity of each to each. This is strictly speaking *the* Marriage Vow; the one essential promise among monogamous races.

But the entrance into this bond brings the contracting parties so much more closely together than any other human connection, that it follows that they ought to afford *primary Benevolence* to one another, and seek each other's welfare before all others; reservation being

7

made of the rights of those to whom they already owe
debts not annullable by the new contract. Most properly
and wisely then, a second promise,—to " honour and
cherish " each other, in sickness and health, poverty and
riches, is, almost universally, added to the original
simple vow of Fidelity. The obligation is acknow-
ledged and reinforced by the vow; but it arises
independently from the nature of the relationship.

A third vow of the wife is added by the English
Church, and by many other Churches—namely, the
Vow of Conjugal *Obedience.* Of this I shall speak in
its turn.

All the world acknowledges the sanctity of the first
of these vows, emphatically in the case of the wife.
The offence of Adultery, which is the infraction of
the vow, if no longer judicially punished in Europe as it
once was, is yet commonly visited by the penalties
of social ostracism. Long may this so continue! Many
of you will think me harsh for saying it; but it is my
deliberate opinion that when a woman has committed
the enormous double crime, personal and social, of
violating the law of chastity, and doing her husband
the mortal wrong of breaking her marriage oath,—
it is fit and right that the society which she has
outraged should close its doors to her. Of this we
shall say more hereafter.

Passing now to the pleasanter subject of the Duty
of Wives to give *special and primary Benevolence* to
their husbands (and vice versa), we meet of course the

invariable obligation to seek first the Moral Good of the
object of our Benevolence. Wives cannot be generally
charged with neglecting the *religious* interests of their
husbands, as they understand them. On the contrary, I
fear, they often worry them about believing what they
consider necessary to salvation, in an unreasoning way
which prevents thoughtful husbands from seeking with
their pious wives that refreshment of spiritual life which
they would find were not all these dogmas in the way.
But the higher *moral* good of the husband occupies most
wives comparatively little ; and often a man who starts
with a great many lofty and disinterested aspirations, de-
teriorates year by year in a deplorable manner under
the influence of a sufficiently well-meaning and person-
ally conscientious wife. If you ask, how can this be ? the
answer is, that the wife's affection, being of a poor and
short-sighted kind, she constantly urges her husband
to think of himself and his own interests, rather than
of the persons and objects for which he was ready to
sacrifice himself. " Do not go on that charitable errand
to-day, you have caught a cold. It will answer as well
to-morrow." " Do not invite that dull old friend."
" Do not join that tiresome committee." " Pray take a
long holiday." " By all means buy yourself a new
hunter." " Do refrain from confessing your unorthodox
opinions." This kind of thing, dropped every day like
the lump of sugar into the breakfast cup of tea, in the
end produces a real constitutional change in the man's
mind. He begins to think himself, first, somewhat of

7 *

a hero when he goes against such sweet counsel ;—and then a Quixote—and then a fool. And a curious reciprocity is also established. The husband cannot do less than return the wife's kindness by begging *her* not to distress and tire herself by performing any duty which costs a little self-sacrifice ; and she again returns the compliment and so on, and so on, till they nurse each other into complete selfishness. I am sure that many of my audience must have seen this exemplified. But if, on the other hand, the wife from the first cherishes every spark of generous feeling or noble and disinterested ambition in her husband, and he, in his turn, encourages her in every womanly charity and good deed, how they will act and re-act on each other month after month and year after year ; each growing nobler, and loving more nobly, and being more worthy to be loved, till their sacred and blessed union brings them together to the very gates of heaven! That is what marriage ought to be ; what it *is* to a few choice and most happy couples ; and what it might be to all.

I should like to have said much on the many ways in which, I think, enlightened moral ideas might help wives to make their husbands more *Happy*, but I can detain you only to name one of them. Tact is an excellent thing, a precious gift to cultivate where it can be used with perfect openness and honesty. But it is one of the worst consequences of the subjection of women, that, in thousands of cases, this tact is developed into the Art of Managing-a-Husband.

Manœuvres, crafty ways, wily little concealments, insidious flatteries and coaxings with an object ; these are the miserable and disgraceful means by which many a well-meaning wife and mother is driven to carry out the most innocent plans, the most useful projects for the family welfare and her children's education. Do not fall into them, my friends ! Do not, whatever be the difficulties of your position, descend to such arts. You may think you make your husband happy by " managing " him so cleverly for his good ; but you may depend on it, though his thick masculine brain does not detect Monday's little *ruse* nor Tuesday's small circumvention, yet that he has a constant and uneasy sense that he is not treated openly and in an above-board fashion, and that you are " too deep " for him. He at once mistrusts, fears and despises such a wife. The whole sincerity of the married life is spoiled ; and in short, whatever number of tricks you may score, you actually *lose the game·* If you could *win* it a hundred times over, it would not be worth degrading yourself into a domestic Mrs. Machiavelli for the purpose !

But now opens upon us the very *crux* of our subject —the third vow which a wife makes when married by the rites of the Church of England or those of most other Churches—the promise to *Obey*.

Of course a reason must be forthcoming for demanding such a vow, though we may privately

suspect that all such reasons did not precede, but
follow, the simple fact; and that wheresoever *la loi du
plus fort* prevails, wives are compelled to obey; and
the vow only adds a mental fetter to the already
existing natural chain, and registers a *fait accompli*.

Some people tell us that it is incumbent on a woman
to take and keep this vow, because she is exhorted by
St. Paul to "obey her husband in the Lord." I
cannot fairly argue this point, being too far outside
the pale of orthodoxy to consider a moral problem to
be solvable by a text. But I would remind those
who quote this passage in one Epistle of the great
Apostle, to remember that they are bound to attach
the same authority to a parallel passage in another
Epistle, wherein the same Apostle commands *Slaves*
to obey their Masters; and actually sends back to his
chain a runaway who in our day would have been
helped to freedom by every true Christian man or
woman in America. The whole tone of early Christian teaching, indeed, was one of entire submission to
the "powers that be," even when they were represented by such insane despots as Tiberius, Caligula
and Nero. In our day, men habitually set aside this
Apostolic teaching, so far as it concerns Masters and
Slaves, Despots and their Subjects, as adapted only
to a past epoch. I am at a loss to see by what right,
having done so, they can claim for it authority when
it happens to refer to Husbands and Wives.

Next to cutting the knot by Authority, I believe

the advocates of Obedience rest their argument on
Expediency—an expediency they think almost amount-
ing to a Necessity, and sanctioned by the practice of
ages. "How can two walk together except they be
agreed?" was a pertinent question of old; but "How
can two walk together *unless one of them have it
entirely his own way?*" is the query put to us by
these persons now. They have become so accustomed
to the notion of one ruling and the other obeying,
that any other kind of arrangement seems to them
fraught with peril of domestic anarchy. My dear
Friends ! Will you please to tell me did you ever hear
of any sort of despotism, great or small, spiritual or
temporal, public or private, which was not justified
by those who exercised it on these same grounds of
its expediency, its convenience, its necessity for the
benefit and safety of the governed? Does not the
Church of Rome exert its tremendous sway over the
intellects and consciences of men, in the honest
persuasion of its hierarchs that it is good for these
sheep to be entirely guided by their shepherds?
Has not every empire in history been founded on
the presumption that one supreme and irresponsible
Ruler or Autocrat could govern a nation much better
than a nation could govern itself? Nay, has it not
been the work of ages, not yet accomplished, to make
mankind understand that all the benefits and con-
veniences of a paternal Government are too dearly
bought by keeping the nations in perpetual childhood?

How is a Church to go on without a supreme Head to determine doctrines? How is a State to go on without a despotic ruler at the helm? How is a Household to go on without an Autocrat to settle all questions by his simple volition? These questions are all very much on a par. Nay, it *ought* surely to be much easier for a little household, united by the tenderest ties, to "get along" peacefully, harmoniously and prosperously as a miniature Republic, than for Churches to flourish on Congregational principles, or States to rise to glory and prosperity, like that of our blessed England—on the basis of some millions of independent wills.

Again; after Authority, and after Expediency and Necessity, Obedience is vindicated by some persons on quite another ground, *not* its utility to the family generally, or to the State, but its *comfort to the obeying party*; the relief it offers to her conscience; the short cut it affords for getting rid of her " responsibilities."

Now I fear I must have a dreadfully hardened conscience, for it has never once occurred to me in life that my responsibilities were things which, (if I could only induce somebody to marry me,) might thus be slipped off and laid aside like old shoes. *What* responsibilities, I ask, are they which I could get rid of, if I were not a wretched "failure," and had a husband to love, honour and *obey*? For example—If I saw a child drowning in a pond, and my husband said, " Don't pick it out of the water on any account;" should I get rid of my " responsibility " by sweetly taking my spouse's arm and walking away, saying, " Just as you think right, dear John " ? Of course, by the law of England, if John had thrown the child into the pond himself, and I stood by aiding and abetting him, I should be held scot free, as acting under marital authority; but I scarcely fancy that my conscience would be altogether relieved of the sense of " Responsibility."

Or again, a much commoner case. I have an old Aunt, we will suppose, a very tiresome person, (as elderly Aunts I find, alas ! are generally considered to be ;) but she was infinitely good to me when I was a child, and I owe her a debt of gratitude which I can never repay. Now she is old and deaf and stupid, and bores my husband to extinction, and he forbids me to invite her to our house, or give her the little cheer and comfort which her lonely old age can receive. Shall I get rid of my " responsibility " towards poor old Aunt Dorothy by writing her a little note and telling her, " I am sorry to observe that my husband wishes me to drop you, and of course it is my duty to obey " ? Here again (and in short, in every imaginable case of a crime to be avoided or a duty to be performed), I find there is no getting rid of that Man of the Sea on my shoulders, viz., Responsibility. My husband or father *cannot* take it off for me, even if we both desire it. And why ? For this reason, my friends ! Because GOD has laid it on me, when He made me a Rational Free

Agent, not a Dog, or an Idiot! No vow I can take
at any altar can make it thereafter Right for me to do
Wrong, or Wrong to do what is Right. There may be
sin *in making the vow*—I believe there would be sin in
making any vow which should make it *more difficult*
for me thenceforward always to do right; but no form
of oath can bind me *not* to do it, any more than
Herod's rash vow ought to have bound him to cut off
the Baptist's head.

Let us then clear this matter away. Responsibilities,
in the sense of moral answerability, cannot be shifted
from one to another on any plea of Obedience after
the human being has reached the age of full moral
accountableness. You will bear in mind this latter
definition. In the case of filial obedience, the *young*
girl must justly defer to the moral *judgment* of her
parents (rather than to their *authority*,) in all save the
most obvious matters of right and wrong. I suppose
even the greatest stickler for parental authority would
admit that if a parent bade a child to steal, he ought
not to obey.

What, then, are the responsibilities which *can* be de-
posited in a husband's or parent's hands? They can
only be those which concern matters *not moral*; matters
concerning the pecuniary or other interests of the family.
On a great many of such points the husband will
usually be wisest, and may most properly be treated
as Mr. Mill suggests, as the Senior, or Acting Partner
in the Firm. And if things go wrong, bad invest-

ments be chosen, and so on, and the wife finds it
any comfort to remark afterwards, that all the *Responsibility* rested with Mr. Smith, and that she had
entirely washed her hands of it—by all means let her
soothe herself with such consolation!   Probably,
however, if she be an able and sensible woman, she
will have preferred to incur the "responsibility" of
strongly advising Mr. Smith not to invest in Egyptian
bonds or Peruvian mines.

Still more will it be impossible for any *mother*, I
should think, to relinquish any control she may
possess over her children's nurture and education
by way of relieving herself of "Responsibility."   It
would be little consolation when Charley has broken
his neck, and Edith is in her coffin, that she had left
with their father the whole " Responsibility," of taking
Charley out riding on a vicious hunter, and bringing
Edith to visit a family in scarlatina.

I cannot pursue these arguments in defence of the
principle of Conjugal Obedience.   To me that principle
seems irreconcileable with the fundamental basis of
morality (namely, the full and independent moral
responsibility of every adult human being) ; and (I
may add) antagonistic no less to the very nature of
that Love and Affection which it is so foolishly
supposed to guarantee.   *Love* naturally reverses the
idea of obedience, and causes the struggle between
any two people who truly love each other to be not who
shall *command*, but, who shall *yield*.   There is in

the world no harder duty than to oppose the will of our heart's best friend. I would go further, and remind you of a beautiful and wise couplet of Chaucer, which somehow has been repeated almost verbally by Spenser (Spenser, of the *Fairy Queen*; not him of *First Principles !*), a couplet I advise you all to commit to memory :—

> " When mastery cometh, then sweet Love anon
> Flappeth his nimble wings and soon away is flown."

It is an insult, a wrong, a deadly wound to Love, for one of the lovers to turn round on the other and claim, not the sweet right to *serve*, but the bitter right to command and control. Practically, we know, in happy marriages this claim rarely crops to the surface ; but the mere fact that it is *sous-entendu* in any discussion seems to me to take the bloom off conjugal love.

Nor are the actual consequences of this doctrine anything short of disastrous. We see one class of wives, of noble, free natures, fretted and galled all their lives by the fetters which some mean-souled man causes to clank whenever he is in an ill-temper. On the other side, we see another set of women who become perfectly passive and silly and " sweetly dependent ; " and at sixty, when their husbands die, they are no better able to manage their own affairs than they were at six, but betray by their childishness that the whole moral work of life has been stopped

for them for half a century. My father (who highly
approved of wifely obedience) used, nevertheless, to
laugh at such widows, and said they reminded him
of clocks with the weights taken off, which instantly
set off buzz, buzz, buzz, till they ran down!

Are the *husbands* any the better or the happier for
this monstrous idea, that they have a right to their
wives Obedience? Certainly not. It cannot and does
not fail to encourage their worst faults of selfishness
and despotism, and to inspire them with contemptuous
ideas of the very woman whom it ought to be the joy
and *elevation* of their souls to honour. When a man
does really honour his wife, we see how beautiful and
happy is their married life; but he does it in sheer
despite of their legal relation, and a very hard achieve-
ment it must be to honour a person who is actually
bound body and soul, for life, to obey your orders; and
whose very children are not hers but yours, to tear
from her arms if you think fit! How many of the
awful crimes perpetrated daily in England by brutal
husbands against their wives would never have been
committed had not the ruffians been taught by law
and custom to regard their wives as their obedient
servants,—their property,—we cannot compute; but I
am convinced that such outrages on women, such wife-
torture and wife-murder, will never cease till the
whole notion of wifely subjection be radically changed.

I cannot pursue these arguments respecting
obedience further; but will simply rehearse the con-

clusions which we seem to have reached on the matter.

Adult human beings, whether men or women, owe *Special Benevolence*,—that is, *Special Service*,—to those persons to whom they are bound either by ties of Birth, of Gratitude, or of Contract. These *Services* may be so far before all others that, while those persons need them, they are bound to pay them before seeking to benefit any other human beings. As a part of such service it is their duty to yield pleasantly and easily in all the small affairs and habits of life; to be perfectly unselfish, affectionate and considerate; and never to thwart or oppose the other unnecessarily. They are also bound to listen to the counsels and wishes of father or mother, husband or wife, not only with courtesy and patience, but with an honest wish to agree with them, and meet them if it be possible.

Beyond this, no adult human being ought to go in the direction of Obedience. To do so would be, not *Service*, but *Slavery*, or the immoral Obedience of the Jesuit to his Superior; a *Moral Suicide*, not to be justified on any plea, whether of authority or precedent, or expediency, or comfort.

If Marriage *necessarily* involved any such Obedience and abnegation of moral responsibility, then I should hold that it was not lawful for any woman to marry; just as I think it is not lawful for any man to become a Jesuit and take his vow of Obedience. But, of course, this is the very matter of our present contention. It is

not in the least necessary, that the Marriage oath,—
which ought to be a reciprocal Promise of Fidelity, and
a reciprocal Promise of Special Benevolence,—should
have superadded to it, a vow that one of the parties
is to be thenceforth, not only *devoted to the other's
welfare*, but *obedient to his will*.

But if Moral Freedom be, as I have tried to show,
so sacred and solemn a charge that we must *never* lay
it aside even for the closest and tenderest human ties,
how great is the obligation which lies on us to use it
aright ! How monstrous would be the position of any
woman who should claim her exemption from filial or
conjugal obedience on the strength of her moral
responsibilities—and then should exhibit in her selfish,
idle, useless, or worldly life, an utter ignorance or
disregard of all which those awful responsibilities to God
involve ! No, my friends ! Better a thousand times
remain the most servilely obedient of wives in perpetual
childhood and dependence, than claim your rank as
Human Beings, Moral Free Agents ; and then show
yourselves no better than monkeys and parrots, or
wilful, self-indulgent children !

You must awake, if you mean to be the pioneers of
a nobler career for your sex, to the charge which lies on
you not to use your liberty for a cloak for licence.
There are women who call themselves " emancipated "
now, who are leading lives, if not absolutely vicious, yet
loose, unseemly, trespassing always on the borders
of vice ; women who treat lightly, and as if of small

account, the heinous and abominable sins of unchastity
and adultery.   For God's sake, my young friends,
beware of such women!   Shun them and repudiate
them as representations of any emancipation which you
desire to share.   Whether in the highest ranks, among
the " fast " ladies of fashion, with their indecorous and
undignified habits, (smoking with the men of their
society at night in smoking-rooms, and so on); or, in
the middle class, the Bohemianism which, to young girl-
students, seems so enchanting after the plodding ways
of home,—in both, this pseudo-emancipation is equally
to be condemned and denounced as having absolutely
nothing in common with the movement for the true
progress of women.

Beside the duties arising from the great formal
Contract of Marriage, there are undoubtedly others
arising from the informal and tacit contract of *Friendship*.   In the older Greek Church and among the
Bedouins there are regularly appointed rites to
solemnize the mutual adoption of Friends.   Such
ceremonies, however, are by no means indispensable to
give sacredness to the bond of every true and noble
friendship of the closer sort ; or to elevate its offices
of fidelity and mutual service to the rank of moral
obligations.   I shall return to this subject a little
further on.

Duties of Women as Mistresses of Households.

After treating of Duties arising from Blood-Relationship, and from the Contract of Marriage and Friendship we come to treat of the Duties which concern us, women, when we are MISTRESSES of HOUSE-HOLDS; and to begin, I must say at once that I have no sympathy at all with those ladies who are seeking to promote co-operative housekeeping, in other words to abolish the institution of the English Home. There may be indeed, specially gifted women, artists, musicians, literary women, whom I could imagine finding it an interruption to their pursuits to take charge of a house. But, strange to say, though I have had a pretty large acquaintance with many of the most eminent of such women, I have almost invariably found them particularly proud of their housekeeping, and clever at the performance of all household duties, not excepting the ordering of "judicious" dinners. Not to make personal remarks on living friends, I will remind you that the greatest woman-mathematician of any age, Mary Somerville, was renowned for her good house-keeping; and, I can add from my own knowledge, was an excellent judge of a well dressed *déjeuner* and of choice old sherry; while Madame de Staël, driven by Napoleon from her home, went about Europe, as it was said, "Preceded by her reputation, and followed by her cook!"

Rather I suspect, it is not higher genius, but feeble inability to cope with the problems of domestic govern-

ment, which generally inspires the women who wish
to abdicate their little household thrones. Some
sympathy may be given to them, but I should be
exceedingly sorry to see many women catching up the
cry and following their leading to the dismal *disfran-
chisement* of the home,—the practical homelessness of
American boarding houses or Continental *pensions*.
I think for a woman to fail to make and keep a happy
home, is to be a "failure" in a truer sense than to
have failed to catch a husband.

Assuredly the Englishwoman's Home is the Englishwoman's Kingdom, and those homes, with all their
faults and shortcomings, are the glory of our country ;
better glories, I think, than if we could transport the
Louvre and St. Mark's, or St. Peter's itself across
the Channel. Out of the English home has sprung
much of that which is most excellent in the national
character ; and with the abolition of it would follow,
I cannot doubt, a dissipation of childhood, and a
loosening of family ties, whereof the evil consequences
would be measureless. Let me entreat you then,
while doing all you can to amend the many and serious
defects which cling around our home system, to lift no
hand to break it down. Make your homes better and
happier and freer than they are, but do not even
speak of the alternative of forsaking them and turning
ourselves into Bedoweens of the lodging house.
For Englishmen, such a change would be very
injurious ; for women, it would be simply disastrous.

The making of a true Home is really our peculiar and

inalienable right; a right which no man can take from
us, for a Man can no more make a Home than a drone
can make a hive. He can build a castle or a palace,
but, poor creature! be he wise as Solomon and rich as
Crœsus, he cannot turn it into a Home. No masculine
mortal can do that. It is a woman, and only a woman;
a woman all by herself if she likes, and without
any man to help her, who can turn a House into a
Home. Woe to the wretched man who disputes her
monopoly, and thinks, because he can arrange a Club,
he can make a Home! Nemesis overtakes him in his
old bachelorhood, when a home becomes the supreme
ideal of his desires; and we see him—him who
scorned the home-making of a *Lady*,—obliged to put
up with the oppression of his cook, or the cruelty of
his nurse!

But it is our privilege, our faculty, to turn any four
walls, nay even a tent under which we take shelter as
we wander about the plains of the East, into a Home, if
we so please it. And shall we relinquish the use of
this blessed faculty, and be content henceforth, like
mere men, to be only quartered here or there, not to
be at home anywhere? Why even the little beavers,
left in a drawing-room, set about making a dam,—a
beaver's Home, out of the coal-scuttle and the rug and
the fire-irons! Shades of our grandmothers keep us
from such degeneracy.

But not to pursue this spectre, let us take our stand
pro aris et focis, and see what Duties belong to us in

right of our Home-Rule. (We, women, are the true
Home Rulers, Parnell and Co. are impostors.)

In the first place, if Home be our kingdom, it must
be our joy and privilege to convert that domain, as
quickly and as perfectly as we may, into a little Province
of the Kingdom of God : for remember what I have
said all along; that we may look on all our duties in
this cheering and beautiful light—first to set up
God's kingdom in our own hearts, making them pure
and true and loving; and then to make our homes
little provinces of the same kingdom; and lastly to try
to extend that kingdom through the world; the empire
of Justice, Truth, and Love. We are entirely responsible for our own souls; and very greatly responsible for those of all the dwellers in our homes ; and,
in a lesser way, we are answerable for each widening
circle beyond us. How shall we set about making our
Homes provinces of the Divine Kingdom ?

1st. Nobody must be morally the worse for
living under our roof, if we can possibly help it.
It is the *minimum* of our duties to make sure
that temptations to misconduct or intemperance are
not left in any one's way ; or bad feelings suffered to
grow up ; or habits of moroseness or domineering
formed ; or quarrels kept hot, as if they were toasts
before the kitchen fire. As much as possible, on the
contrary, everybody must be helped to be better,—not
made better by Act of the Drawing Room, remember,
that is impossible,—but *helped* to be better. The way

to do this, I apprehend, is neither very much to scold, or exhort, or insist on people going to church whether they like it or not, or reading Family Prayers, (excellent though that practice may be) but rather to spread through the house such an atmosphere of frank confidence and kindliness with servants, and of love and trust with children and relations, as that bad feelings and doings will really have no place, no temptation, and if they intrude, will soon die out.

One such point out of many I may here cite as specially concerning us women. Is it not absurd for a lady who spends hundreds of pounds and thousands of hours on her toilet, and takes evident pleasure in attracting admiration in fashionable raiment not always perfectly decent—to turn and lecture poor Mary Ann, her housemaid, on sobriety in attire, and set forth to her the peril and folly of flowers in her bonnet? The mistress who dresses modestly and sensibly, may reasonably hope in time that her servants will dress modestly and sensibly likewise; but certainly they will not do so while she exhibits to their foolish young eyes the example of extravagance and folly.

2nd. Next to the *Virtue* of those who live in our homes, their *Happiness* should occupy us. In the first place, no creature under our roof should ever be miserable, if we can prevent it. In how many otherwise happy homes is there not one such miserable being? Sometimes it is the sufferer's own fault: their minds are warped and despairful, and our utmost efforts perhaps can only

cheer them a little. But much oftener there is to be
found in a large household some poor creature who has
fallen, through no fault, into the miserable position of
the family *butt ;* the object of ill-natured and unfeeling
jests and rude speeches; the last person to be given
any pleasure, and the first person to be made to suffer
any privation or ill-temper. Sometimes it is a poor
governess or tutor; sometimes an old aunt or poor
relation ; now and then, but rarely in these days, a stupid
servant ; most often of all, a child, who is perhaps a
step-child, or nephew, or niece of the mistress of the
house, or alas ! her own child, only deformed in some way,
or deficient in intellect. Then the hapless frightened
creature, afraid of punishment, looks with furtive glances
at the frowning faces about it, tries to escape by some
little transparent deception, and only incurs the
heavier penalty of falsehood and the name of a liar ; and
so the evil goes on growing day by day. It is
astonishing and horrible to witness how the deep-seated
frightful human passion, which I have elsewhere
named *Heteropathy,*develops itself in such circumstances
·—the sight of suffering and down-trodden misery exciting, not pity, but the reverse; a sort of cruel *aversion*
in the bystanders, till the whole household sometimes
joins in hating the poor helpless and isolated victim.

My friends, if you ever see anything approaching to
this in your homes, for God's sake set your faces like a
flint against it ! If you dislike and mistrust the poor
victim yourself, as you probably will do at first, never

mind ! Take, my word for it, the first thing to be done
in the Kingdom of God is to do JUSTICE to all,—to
secure that no creature, however mean, or even loath-
some, should be treated with injustice. If you are,
as I am supposing, mistress of the house, stop this
persecution with a high hand ; and if you have been in
any way to blame in it, if it be *your* dislike which you
see thus reflected in the faces of your dependants,
repent your great fault, and make amends to your
victim. If you are not mistress, only a guest perhaps,
or a humble friend, even then you can and ought to
do much ; you can look grave and pained whenever
the butt is laughed at and jeered ; and you can
deliberately fix your eyes on him, or her, with sympathy,
and treat him with respect. Even these little tokens
of condemnation of what is going on will have (you
may be sure), a startling effect on those whose custom
it has become to treat the poor soul with contempt ;
and they will probably be angry with you for exhibiting
them. You will never have borne resentment for a
better cause !

Nor is it only human beings who are thus made too
often household victims. You must all know houses
where some unlucky animal—a cat or dog—beginning
by being the object of somebody's senseless antipathy,
becomes the general *souffre-douleur* of masters and
servants. The dog or cat (especially if it happens to be
cherished by the human victim), is spoken to so
roughly, driven out of every room, and perhaps

punished for all sorts of offences it has never committed, that the animal assumes a downcast, sneaking
aspect, which inevitably produces fresh and fresh
heteropathy. You attempt, perhaps, to give it a little
pat of sympathy, and the poor frightened beast snaps
at you, expecting a blow; or runs off to hide under a
sofa. Mistresses of homes! don't let there be a dog,
or a cat, or a donkey, or any other creature, in or
about your homes, which shrinks when a man or
woman approaches it! And here I may add, that
without thus specially victimizing the animals through
dislike, a household frequently makes the life of some
poor brute one long martyrdom through neglect. The
responsibility for this neglect lies primarily with the
mistress of the house. She must not only direct her
servants, but *see that her directions be carried out,* in
the way of affording water, and food, and needful
exercise. A pretty "Kingdom of Heaven" some
houses would be if the poor brutes could speak; houses
possibly with prayers going on twice a day, and grace
said carefully before long luxurious meals,—and all the
time the children's birds and rabbits left untended in
foul cages without fresh food; mice thrown out of the
traps on the fire; aged or diseased cats, or superfluous
puppies given to boys to destroy in any way their cruel
invention may suggest; fowls for the consumption of
the house carelessly and barbarously killed; and, worst
of all, the poor house-dog, perhaps some loving-hearted
little Skye, or noble old mastiff or retriever, con-

demned for life to the penalties which we should
think too severe for the worst of malefactors : chained
up by the neck through all the long bright summer
days under a burning sun, with its water-trough
unfilled for days, or through the winter's frost in some
dark sunless corner, freezing with cold and in agonies
of rheumatism for want of straw or the chance of
warming itself at a fire, or by a run in the snow. And
all this as a reward for the poor brute's fidelity !
When this kind of thing goes on for a certain time, of
course the dog becomes horribly diseased. His longing
to bound over the fresh grass—expressed so affectingly
by his leaps and bounds when we approach his
miserable dungeon,—is not merely a longing for his
natural pleasure, but for that which is indispensable
to his health, namely exercise, and the power to eat
grass ; and, if refused, he very soon falls into disease :
his beautiful coat becomes mangy and red; he is
irritable, and becomes revolting to everybody, and
the nurse cries to the children, who were his only
friends and visitors, " Don't go near that dog !"

I say it deliberately, the mistress of a house in whose
yard a dog is thus kept like a *forçat*—only worse
treated than any murderer is treated in Italy—is guilty
of a *very great sin ;* and till she has taken care that
the dog has his daily exercise and water, and that
the cat and the fowls and every other sentient creature
under her roof is well and kindly treated, she may
as well, for shame's sake, give up thinking she is ful-

filling her duties by reading prayers and subscribing to missions.

I assume that the master of the house, where there is one, will, as usual, look after the stable department. Where there is no master, or he does not interfere, the mistress is surely responsible for humane treatment of the horses, if she keep any. Further, I think every lady is bound to insist that any horse which draws her shall be free from the misery of a bearing-rein. She ought not to allow her vanity and ambition to be fashionable, to induce her to connive at her coachman's laziness and cruelty.

When the Mistress of a house has done all she can to *prevent the suffering*, mental or physical, of any creature, human or infra-human, under her roof, there remains still a delightful field for her ability in actually *giving pleasure*. We all know that life is made up chiefly of little pleasures and little pains; and how many of the former are in the power of the mistress of a house to provide, it is almost impossible to calculate. But let any clever woman simply take it to heart to make everybody about her *as happy as she can*, and the result I believe will always be wonderful. Let her see that so far as possible, they have the rooms they like best, the little articles of furniture and ornament they prefer. Let her order meals with a careful forethought for their tastes, and for the necessities of their health; seeing that every one has what he desires, and making him feel, however humble in position,

that his tastes have been remembered. Let her not
disdain to pay such attention to the position of the
chairs and sofas of the family dwelling-rooms as
that every individual may be comfortably placed,
and feel that he or she has not been left out in the
cold. And after all these cares, let her try, not so
much to make her rooms splendid and æsthetically
admirable, as to make them thoroughly habitable and
comfortable for those who are to occupy them;
regarding their comfort rather than her own æsthetic
gratification. A drawing-room, bright and clean, sweet
with flowers in summer, or with dried rose leaves in
winter; with tables at which the inmates may occupy
themselves, and easy chairs wherever they are wanted;
and plenty of soft light, and warmth, or else of coolness adapted to the weather—this sort of room belongs
more properly to a woman who seeks to make her
house a province of the Kingdom of *Heaven,* than
one which might be exhibited at South Kensington
as having belonged to the Kingdom of *Queen Anne!*

Then for the moral atmosphere of the house, which
depends so immensely on the tone of the mistress; I
will venture to make one recommendation. Let it be
as gay as ever she can make it. There are numbers
of excellent women—the salt of the earth—who seem
absolutely oppressed with their consciences, as if they
were congested livers. They are in a constant state
of anxiety and care; and, perhaps with the addition
of feeble health, find it difficult to get through their

duties except in a certain lachrymose and dolorous fashion. Houses where these women reign seem always under a cloud, with rain impending. Now I conceive that good, and even high animal spirits, are among the most blessed of possessions,—actual wings to bear us up over the dusty or muddy roads of life; and I think that to keep up the spirits of a household, is not only indefinitely to add to its happiness, but also to make all duties comparatively light and easy. Thus, however naturally depressed a mistress may be, I think she ought to struggle to be cheerful, and to take pains never to quench the blessed spirits of her children or guests. All of us who live long in great cities get into a sort of subdued-cheerfulness tone. We are neither very sad nor very glad ; we neither cry, nor ever enjoy that delicious experience of helpless laughter, the *fou rire* which is the joy of youth. I wish we could be more really light of heart.

A few words must suffice upon the vexed question of Servants.

I do not represent to myself a household as a Despotism, so much as a Community, wherein some persons (the servants) have contracted, on certain terms, to perform a certain class of services for the heads of the house, their children and guests. The mistress (it is part of the contract) is authorized to give directions at all moments how those services are to be performed; and she is also authorized (it is understood) to give such further directions respecting the dress and habits of the servants, their hours for coming home, the persons they shall admit into the house, &c., as may appear necessary for the order and safeguard of the house. But with these *directions* I think her claims to *authority* are exhausted. Into the employment of any leisure time her servants may have, and their private affairs generally, she has no right, in virtue of their contract, to intrude at all; and I cannot but think that the recognition of this line of demarcation, the formal relinquishment of the patriarchal relation (which can only now be really maintained in exceptional cases), and the careful observance of the contract, would be the safest, as it is the truest, basis for our future relationship with our servants. When this basis is fairly laid, I think servants can be better brought to respect their side of the contract; to do us just and honest service for honest wages; and, metaphorically and literally, to "sweep under the mats." There remains, outside of their actual service, or of any assumption of authority on our side, an actually limitless field for the exercise of our natural influence as their immediate superiors and friends.

One word in concluding these remarks on Woman's duties as a *Haus Frau.* If we cannot perform these well, if we are not orderly enough, clear-headed enough, powerful enough in short, to fulfil this immemorial function of our sex well and thoroughly, it is somewhat foolish of us to press to be allowed to share in the great Housekeeping of the State. My beloved and honoured friend, Theodore Parker, argued for the admission of women to the full rights of citizenship and share in government, on the express grounds that few women keep house so badly or with such wastefulness as Chancellors of the Exchequer keep the State ; and womanly genius for organization applied to the affairs of the nation would be extremely economical and beneficial. But if we cannot keep our houses, and manage our servants, this argument, I am afraid, will be turned the other way, and we shall be told that *not* having used our one talent, it is quite out of question to give us ten; having shown ourselves incapable in little things, nobody in their senses will trust us with great ones.

LECTURE V.

Duties of Women as Members of Society.

IN the Second Lecture of this Course I spoke of the *Personal Duties* of Women. In the Third Lecture we discussed their *Social Duties* generally, beginning with their Duties as Members of Families, Mothers, Daughters, Sisters, &c. In the Fourth Lecture I spoke of the Duties of Wives and Mistresses of Households. We now come to the consideration of the Duties of a Woman as *a Member of Society*; reserving for our last Lecture her Duties as a Citizen of the State and Member of the Human Race.

In this Lecture I beg you to take note that I shall use the word " Society" in its narrower conventional sense, implying the association of equals for purposes of pleasure, mutual hospitality, visits, entertainments, and so forth. The larger sense of the word " Society," as applied to all human intercourse, is not here intended.

If the Home be, as it is often well called, " Woman's Kingdom," every drawing-room is woman's throne-room. Modern civilized society all proceeds on the

assumption, not only of woman's right to share in
almost all kinds of social pleasures, (a concession
already surprising to an Oriental), but to hold in them,
conventionally, the position of the superior. Practically
we all know that there is a good deal of ko-towing to
men, in drawing-rooms as elsewhere ; but, theoretically,
a woman in society is queen. She may acknowledge
or *cut* her male acquaintance as she sees fit, and every
man is bound to pay her that tribute of little civilities—
bowings, and uncoverings, and openings of doors, and
handing of chairs,—which some foolish women deem so
inexpressibly valuable that they would not have us
lose them for the sake of civil and political equality;
(a choice which reminds me of the fable of the Dog and
the Bone and the Shadow.) This being the case, it
would surely seem that we ought, long ere this time,
to have fulfilled our unquestionable duty and have
made society a good deal better and happier. It is
true that we go to our friends' parties, and invite them
to our own, for pleasure and not to preach morals.
We very properly should eschew the invitation of any
lady who should treat her dinner table as a pulpit;
and I confess I even feel resentful against those good
souls who sometimes come to parties with *malice
prepense*, determined to do philanthropic business;
and spend the time in button-holing one influential
man or woman after another ; asking Mr. A. to vote
for a Deaf and Dumb, and Mrs. B. for an Idiot, and
Miss C. to attend the Committee of the Up-at-Six-

every-Morning Society, and Professor D. to join the
new Association for the Promotion of Perpetual
Ratiocination. This turning of a drawing-room into
a little Benevolence Exchange, is quite unpardonable
I think (though I am afraid I have sometimes been
guilty of it myself). But surely it is not to go thus
into Society on false pretences, to *carry with us into it*
our genuine moral feelings—our love and enjoyment
of " whatsoever things are honest," whatsoever things
are lovely, and kindly, and pure, and true ; and our
disgust and antipathy for whatsoever things are the
reverse ? If instead of the *banal* smile wherewith we
commonly equally greet a fine sentiment or a bit of
true humour, or a pretty story,—and *also* a spiteful
remark, or an anecdote verging on the *scabreux*,—we
were to welcome the first with the sympathy we really
feel, and treat the latter with a coldness which should
effectually mark our disgust, the results in the long run
would be considerable. There is, for example, in almost
every society a *detracting* way (that is the exact word)
of treating absent persons which it behoves every
good-natured woman to check by the simple, well-bred
expedient of merely *looking bored*. Nothing more is
necessary—merely *look bored,* and you will not often
be pestered with this kind of stupid spitefulness.
For once that anybody resorts to it from real malice,
it is twenty times employed by dull, half-cultivated
people as the best way they know of exciting interest
in their chatter.

And once again, I think, it behoves us women to use our immense social influence in utterly discouraging and putting down those attacks upon our sex generally, which in Parliament and in certain newspapers, afford just the same refined and elevated amusement which our ancestors found in the public recreation for which the pious Alleyne liberally contributed, namely, "Whipping of the Blind Bear!" Those debates in Parliament wherein certain facetious speakers distinguish themselves, are they not very like "whipping of the Blind Bear?" We are up in the Ladies' Gallery of the House of Commons, like the bear tied to its stake, unable to deal our tormentors even a dab with our paws, while they are diverting themselves, giving us the heaviest cuts which their cart-whips can inflict. Truly it is a gallant and gentlemanly sport, and one of which it appears these members of Parliament will not soon tire. But is it quite consistent with our dignity as women that the men who say and write these things should be just as welcome to us, just as free to enter our drawing-rooms, as those generous friends who stand by us year after year, and bear for our sakes and the sake of justice, the scoffs and sneers levelled at them as our champions? There is, it seems to me, a terrible want of *esprit de corps* among women; an unmeaning readiness to smile equally at every man, —or perhaps, I ought in some cases to say, rather a base and servile willingness to flatter men by pretending to agree with them in their contempt for the claims of

women. Were women only united in common feeling
and the insult done to the sex generally, felt by every
woman as a wrong and insult to herself, did every
woman say (transposing the old Roman poet's words)
"I am a *Woman*, and nothing which concerns women
is alien to me," then this sort of thing would be put
down very shortly.

But there is a still graver order of offences which I
believe it is the high duty of women to discountenance
by driving out of society those who are guilty of them.
I speak of offences either against the great laws of
Chastity, or of Honesty, or of Humanity; and I
maintain that it is the duty of every woman to refuse
to associate with persons who are notoriously guilty of
them. Remember I say "*notoriously* guilty." It is
not our business to pry into any one's secrets, but
when vices and crimes are secrets no longer, when
men or women stand convicted of Adultery, Seduction,
Swindling, or Cruelty, I insist that they are no longer
fit to join in social pleasures; that their presence
is a blight on them; and that no woman ought either
to receive them in her own house, or consent to meet
them at the entertainments of her friends.

I have been greatly blamed for pronouncing this
judgment; and when I first delivered these Lectures
in London, more than one of my audience treated
me as hard-hearted, and argued that, after a certain
interval had elapsed, such offenders ought to be rein-
stated in their social privileges. It was indeed strange

9 *

to me thus to be accused of harshness, seeing that I
believe none can desire more than I do to treat
tenderly *repentant* guilt of every form,—but most of
all in the piteous form of ruined womanhood. But
the misunderstanding arose from two causes. *I* spoke
of Society exclusively as the scene of social *amusements ;*
my critics insisted on talking of the whole range of
human intercourse. *They* thought of humble and
repentant guilt; while I thought of the spectacle (alas!
much more common) of triumphant and insolent vice,
flaunting itself in every haunt of pleasure. The matter
is of such great importance that you must suffer me to
speak upon it more at length.

It was almost my foremost object in undertaking
the somewhat audacious scheme of addressing my
fellow countrywomen on our Duties, to do all that
might be possible for me to *separate* the sacred cause
of the social and political emancipation of women from
certain modes of thought and action which it has been
the business of false friends and open enemies to con-
found therewith. The preachers of the hateful and
disgusting doctrines of Free-Love have been the bane
and calamity of our allies in America. We have
nothing quite so bad here; but we have, in the highest
circles, a new development of "fastness," very nearly
akin to profligacy, and quite akin to the neglect of all
decorum and womanly dignity; and we have, in the
middle classes, also, a new tone, if not of behaviour
yet of opinion ; a tone of laxity in discussing breaches

of the law of chastity which must prove no less disastrous in its results than it is, in my opinion, erroneous in principle.

We have attempted in these studies (as I may call them) to treat ethical questions as they ought to be treated; namely, with as near an approach as possible to a scientific method; deducing them from principles upon which we have (I hope) all agreed. Now one of the most important of these principles is, that Virtue must always be a *higher end* than Happiness, and that we must never postpone the end of Virtue for the end of Happiness. When, therefore, we are considering a point which must affect closely the moral welfare—the *virtue*—of society at large, I might justly refuse to entertain the plea that it would be more kind, more for the *happiness* of certain erring individuals, that the course best suited to promote that highest end should not be adopted.

But, my Friends! I do not think we need have recourse to this painful alternative between Justice to society and Mercy to offenders; because I hold with uttermost conviction, that it is *not* Mercy, this pseudo-charity, this easy condonation of enormous sin; *not* mercy to the offender himself, whose conscience is falsely soothed and pacified, and who is led into a life hollow and unreal, utterly unfit for his true moral condition,—and the very reverse of mercy to the innocent members of society who have a right to be shielded from the contagion of vice.

I am not now speaking exclusively of sins against Chastity. I have already placed in the same category, great sins of Fraud, and also, emphatically, sins of Cruelty. Let us review, then, once more the question, "How ought society to treat persons notoriously guilty of any enormous sin?" Does mercy or charity ask of us that we should, after a given interval, receive them back into the circle of our social pleasures? Are the amusements of the innocent fitted for souls blasted and marred by crime, and (at the best) seared by the hot iron of remorse? Is admission to such pleasures the proper guerdon of repentance? Bah! Repentance rewarded by invitations to dinner-parties! A broken and a contrite spirit comforted by a card for a ball!

Such quiet intercourse as may be shared in the privacy of their homes is another matter; and is very proper for those who believe they can thereby confer a benefit. But, by the very hypothesis, IF the offender be really repentant, he or she will not seek, but rather shrink from noisy pleasures; and the manifestation of a desire to re-enter the scene of them with a blighted reputation, is nothing else than a betrayal of total callousness and unrepentance.

As to the idea that a limit in *time* could be fixed, after which these social ostracisms should come to an end and the banished persons be re-admitted, and re-habilitated, a sort of *Moral Quarantine*,—I confess it seems to me purely illusive and nugatory. *When* should the Act of Condonation be passed?—

Ought it to be after five years? Or three years? Or one year? Or *one month*? Whatever period might be first adopted, it would inevitably be shortened in one case after another case. The principle that it was merciful and kind to re-admit the sinner being once accepted, nobody would be willing to incur the odium of insisting on a longer banishment. Very soon we should have simply the shortest *eclipse* (little more than the evil honeymoon of vice itself), and then the triumphant offenders would re-appear as the petted returned Prodigals of their circles of acquaintance.

This is not my idea of Mercy; still less is it my idea of *Truth* and straight-forwardness. From the first of these Addresses I have tried to convey to you my sense of the infinite sanctity of Veracity as a Personal Virtue, never to be postponed for any motive of Benevolence or good-nature; and I have exhorted you, with all the power I possessed, to endeavour to make your whole lives straight-forward, and all your social intercourse simple and upright,—to be *dans le vrai* in all your relations. What, then, shall we say of the appeal to us to treat great and notorious offenders as they must be treated if they are to be restored to society at all,—that is, with respectful courtesy, and cheerful cordiality? Certainly nobody can wish them to be brought back to be met with "the cold shoulder" of contempt. The tone of society must be uniformly courteous, and they must benefit by it *if* they enter society at all. But how are we, consistently with any veracity, any self-respect, any straight-forwardness —to treat swindlers, and adulterers, and men guilty of hideous cruelties, with respect or cordiality ? If I must smile at the smooth jests of the fraudulent director; and shake the hand which an hour ago was engaged in the devilish work of animal-torture; and treat as " hail fellow, well met " the profligate destroyer of the happiness of a family—then society must be for me one huge sham and falsehood, a dismal piece of play-acting in a dull farce; and I should beg to renounce it for ever, and expect every honest man and woman to do the same. I will *not*—I say it deliberately, I will *not*, for any good-nature, or even any mercy,—supposing it to *be* mercy,—act a living lie, pretend to treat as friends the men and women whose deeds I loathe, and pay the semblance of honour to those to whom I know that honour is *not* due. I will not laugh and exchange the comradeship of an innocent jest, with men over whose deeds angels might weep and God must frown; I will not pollute my hand by placing it, knowingly, in that of a villain.

Turn we now from the vice and wrong which women as members of society are bound to discountenance to the Virtue and Happiness they may assist.

My great panacea for making Society at once better and more enjoyable would be to cultivate greater *sincerity*. In my second Lecture I spoke of Veracity as a great Personal Virtue. I left its discussion as a Social Duty, *i.e.* its secondary and minor obligation, for this occasion.

A great many well-meaning persons are puzzled between the rival claims of veracity and politeness in ordinary social intercourse, and we see some manifestly postponing veracity to what they consider to be the demands of politeness, and becoming odious flatterers; and others postponing politeness to what they think the demands of veracity, and becoming insufferably rude and brusque. It is not then useless to try and get at the real moral principles which ought to decide our conduct in every case wherein the two principles seem to clash.

I must remind you here of what I remarked before, that *words have no absolute meaning;* their meaning is the sense which we agree,—speaker and hearer,—to attach to them. To speak truly, is to speak so that the person we address shall understand the truth. To speak falsely is to speak so that he may be deceived. It is the intention and effort to deceive wherein alone lie the guilt and disgrace of lying. Bearing this obvious rule in mind you will see at once that, in every language, a considerable number of phrases are used, not in a literal but a conventional sense, and can deceive, and are intended to deceive nobody. We sign our letters " Yours truly," without in the least intending to signify that we *belong,* in any sense whatever, to the person we address. Our grandfathers wrote, they were their correspondents' "humble and obedient servants," when they were neither "humble" nor "obedient," nor their "servants" in any sense. A Spaniard assures you his house belongs to you, but would be very indignant if you took him at his word for a farthing rushlight. An Italian addresses you as "Pregiatissima," and subscribes himself your "Divotissimo," without anybody supposing you are "most prized," or he "most devoted." To what then, do all these phrases amount? Simply to expressions of *courtesy;* and when you use them, if you mean to be *courteous,* you are perfectly truthful. There is no deception and no intention to deceive. Once for all, then, let us set apart all phrases which are in common use as conventional expressions of civility, and recognize that there can be no infraction of the laws of veracity in using them in the ordinary way.

But now comes the pinch! Women who are of a "gushing" disposition, or very anxious to ingratiate themselves with others, are exceedingly apt to overleap these conventional phrases of courtesy and make use of other terms which are *not* conventional, but are commonly employed in their natural sense as expressions of much stronger sentiments,—sincere affection, or respect, or gratitude; real joy, or genuine sorrow. They *write* these words and they *act* them; they press the hand tenderly where courtesy requires only a bow or an ordinary shake of the hand; or they kiss,—an act which nobody short of the Queen is bound to do except from genuine sentiment. Can there be any doubt that here is falsehood, in every case wherein the woman does not genuinely feel more than courtesy,—some real affection, or respect or sympathy? A great deal of this kind of thing is done by women; and has gained for our sex a bad name for sincerity. I do not think it is always so insincere as it seems; or that it is always a Judas-kiss which one woman offers in public to another of whom she is not particularly fond. It is more often, I think, the habit of exaggerating everything they say and do into which weak persons are very apt to fall; just as all weak writers affect strong language and heap up epithets to give intensity to washy sentences. But the evil is considerable, and must always be an offence against strict simplicity and sincerity, even if it do not amount to intentional deception. Thus I would urge every woman who has any tendency to this kind of thing to overhaul her vocabulary, and make up her mind which phrases she may safely use as mere conventional courtesies, and which others (including her kisses) she must reserve to express only her genuine sentiments.

Be true, my friends, I implore you,—true to yourselves,—true in your family relations,—true in society. Believe that old Chaucer said well :—

"Truth to thine own heart thy soul shall save."

Go through life straight ahead, fearing nothing so much as to incur the deadly disgrace of crooked ways, and flattering words, and false-hearted caresses, and

mean stratagems and manœuvres. The day in which
women renounce all these basenesses, and learn to
resent the imputation of them as a mortal insult, will
be a better day for us than the one which sees our
political emancipation.

I shall say no more now of the special ways in which
women may use their power to purify and amend
society. If a woman be herself pure and noble-hearted,
she will come into every circle as a person does into a
heated room who carries with him the freshness of
the woods where he has been walking—"the smell
of the field which the Lord hath loved."

There is one general principle which may, perhaps,
better be insisted on here than anywhere else. It is
this: that in our whole social intercourse with our
fellows—in the family, the home, in society, and in all
public work—the power of any individual to do good
must depend almost, measure for measure, on the
extent of that individual's power of sympathy—the
wideness and the warmth of his heart. The power of
thinking,—the capacity of his *head*, is but a secondary
matter. I have often quoted before, and I cannot
repeat too often the words of a man who, himself, most
marvellously united the great heart and the strong
head, the late dear and venerable Matthew Davenport
Hill. "It is difficult," he said, "to estimate sufficiently the *aggressive* power of love and kindness."
That is the true word, the aggressive, the invasive, the
irresistible, tide-like power swelling up through every

stream and rivulet—of love and kindness. Never think, —you who are young, and glorying perhaps in the grand new fields of intellectual culture opened before you, that the Intellect is nobler than the Heart—that Knowledge is greater than Love. Not so! A thousand times no! The vilest of beings,—*devils*, if there were such creatures,—might very easily *know* more than all the men of science in Europe put together; and *be* devils at the end of it, with every cruelty, every baseness and bitterness in their miserable souls. Mephistopheles knew a great deal more than Faust— Claude Bernard than the dog he tortured; but Faust was nobler than his Tempter, the dog than the physiologist. It is here, in the faculty of noble, disinterested, unselfish love, that lies the true gift and power of our womanhood; the power which makes us,—not the *equals* of men (I never care to claim such equality), but their *equivalents*; more than their equivalents in a moral sense. This is the God-like thing in human nature, the Divine breath of the higher life; and it is "in this sign," the sign of self-sacrificing Love wherein we conquer.

In picturing then, the ideal life of woman in her Home and in Society, I should utterly fail if I did not convey to you my sense, that it must be supremely a *loving life*—a life of tender, multiform, perennial sympathy with the pleasures and sorrows of all around her; and of the deep joy of fervent personal affection. I can imagine nothing more miserable, no

social life a more wretched failure, than that of a
certain lady in London of whom I have heard it said
that she has "five hundred people on her visiting list,
and not a friend among them." My ideal of life would
be very different from this. It would be first, the
closest love of *one*; then true and tender affection for
many; then kindly good-will to *all*.

I think that everyone, at least some time or other
in life, must have the chance offered to them of forming a true marriage with one of the opposite sex, or
else a true friendship with one of their own; and that
we should look to such marriages and friendships as
the supreme joy and glory of mortal life; unions
wherein we may'steep our whole hearts; love such as
that of which some poet says that it—

> " Like an indivisible glory lay on both our souls,
> And dwelt in us, as we did dwell in it."

This is our natural inheritance of comfort and
delight, of which we need scarcely be cheated save by
our own fault. We women, have been always told to
look for it in Marriage; and truly I believe (indeed
it is impossible to doubt), that in a thoroughly happy
and worthy marriage, it must be realized in its uttermost perfection. But I think it is time (especially
now, when a fourth of the women in this country never
marry, and considering, also, that a woman cannot
seek to marry the man who might best fill her heart),
to let all women from girlhood bear in mind, that,
although a perfect marriage be *a* perfect ideal of

Friendship, it is not the *only* form in which friendships can be perfected; nor the only relation in life
wherein the demands of our hearts can be fulfilled.
There are, I suppose, some women (rather perhaps of
the clinging order) whose natures could never find
their complement or be quite satisfied, except in
Marriage, and for these I can only wish—a good
husband! But if I am not mistaken, there are a considerable number who are capable of being quite as
completely satisfied by Friendship; and not a few
whose dispositions are such that they are better suited
for Friendship than for Marriage; women of the
character described by Emerson as the true types of
friends, who do not need to *lean*, but to *clasp hands*
along the journey of life. More and more, I expect, as
time goes on, women who have not the blessing of
sisters who can live with them, will form these life-long
sisterly friendships with other women; and find in them
the affection and the comradeship which will fill their
hearts and cheer all their later years.

And then, beyond such closest and most enduring
bonds, there lie open in this rich world to every loving
heart the most wonderful variety and wealth of possible
friendships; with old and with young; with our contemporaries and with children; with men and with
women; with the wise and good and great, to whom
we look up with tender reverence; and with the pure
and fresh young creatures who cling around us, like
honeysuckles round a gnarled old tree.

Social Duty, in short, my Friends, as we were taught long ago, is summed up in the Second Commandment of the Law. *Love,* in the Family, in the Home, in Society, and in the World is " the fulfilment of the Law ;" and there is no fulfilling any law, however small, of social duty without it. He or she who leads a thoroughly loving life, not only " lives in God ;" but shares something of God's own power to move and bless the world.

LECTURE VI.

——◆——

Woman as a Citizen of the State.

THE share which women have hitherto been permitted to take in the public affairs of nations has singularly oscillated. Our sex always seems to be in the zenith or at the nadir; on the throne or nowhere; at the goal or out of the running. There have been two or three dozen great female rulers in universal history, and the proportion of able and prosperous sovereigns among them, compared to the proportion of similarly able and prosperous Monarchs among the many hundreds of kings, is a most astonishing fact. Semiramis, Nitocris, Artemisia, Deborah, Zenobia, Cleopatra, Boadicea, Elizabeth, Isabella of Castile, Maria Theresa, Catherine the Great, Anne and Victoria—many of these women, semi-fabulous or historical, virtuous or vicious, were yet, to all seeming, so gifted with the special *governing* faculty that they have each made an epoch in history; while France, the only country in Europe which has held to the Salic law and refused to admit a lawful Queen Regnant, has been punished by

10

Nemesis in the shape of a score of female harpies, Diane de Poitiers, Madame de Pompadour, Madame du Barry, *et hoc genus omne.*

Mr. Mill says that when he was at the India House he observed that whenever a province in India was particularly well governed by a native prince, he found, in three cases out of four, that it was some *woman,* some Begum or Ranee who had emerged from the Zenana to wield the sceptre with a vigour and good sense rarely paralleled among the Rajahs. At this moment our ablest and most faithful ally among the native princes in India is a woman; while Ranavalona, Queen of Madagascar, is the paragon of African sovereigns, as Pomare was, in her time, of Polynesian chiefs.

Historians when they deign to notice this curious preponderance of ability among female rulers have been wont to explain it in a way delightfully soothing to masculine pride. They say that a queen is well guided by her male ministers; while a king is too often misguided by bad female favourites. I will only remark that the power of *choosing* able ministers is the very first qualification of a sovereign, and that, unluckily for the theory, a great number of the most prosperous queens kept the reins tightly in their own hands and employed Secretaries rather than Ministers. On the other hand, a king who chooses bad favourites and allows himself to be guided by them, appears to exhibit the very worst and most mischievous weakness which could beset a sovereign.

Again, beside the great Queens we find all down the stream of history when a nation has been involved in extreme peril, it has happened that some woman, some Jael or Judith or Esther, some Maid of Saragossa or of Orleans, steps forth and saves the situation; and she has been duly lauded for her heroism to the skies, though occasionally left by her chivalrous countrymen to be burned at the stake.

But between these heights of royalty and heroism and the abasement of political non-entity, there seems to be no *mezzo termine* for our unfortunate sex. *Public Spirit* is a quality which we are not encouraged to cultivate, and it is almost by a figure of speech that I have spoken of our duties as Citizens of the State. The dignity of citizenship (as understood by the old Romans, for example) certainly included more than *our* particular privilege—namely, that of paying all the taxes without possessing any corresponding rights! It has been assumed that not only should a woman's charity begin at home but stop there; or, at the most, make the round of the parish under the direction of the parson, distributing tracts and soup tickets.

But at last, womanly charity and public spirit have broken their bounds. An immense breach was made in the invisible hedges wherewith our mothers and grandmothers were surrounded within the memory of many of us, when Miss Nightingale and the late regretted Mary Stanley went out to the Crimea to nurse the soldiers. Mary Carpenter also, of blessed memory,

10 *

managed by sheer dint of volition and continually acting the Widow to the Unjust Judge, and with the help of Recorder Hill and others, to force so many legislative reforms through Parliament and cut such a quantity of masculine red tape,—that M.P.'s and heads of Departments began to recognize women's ideas as things which might actually deserve attention. Mr. Stansfeld (all honour to him from all of us!) took a step which would have led to indefinitely important results had he remained in office,—in appointing the first woman to an office of public trust under Government; *that* woman being the beloved and admirable Mrs. Nassau Senior. Then came the School-Board elections and representation ; by far the greatest bound forward our cause has made. Who would have thought, —my dear *Contemporaries* here present!—who would have thought, when you and I were young, that we should live to see the day when elections of women, for what is practically a great Civil Parliament, should be going on now all over England ; and everywhere with such extraordinary and triumphant success that the newspapers complain peevishly of the useless waste of votes in showing how determined the electors are to return female candidates ! The possession of votes for municipal elections and the occasional election of women (like the excellent Miss Merrington) as Guardians of the Poor, are also vast strides in the direction of public usefulness for women. Further, as on the safe-guard and basis of the whole movement we have the

enormous improvement, I might call it revolution,
which has been made of late years in the education of
women,—fitting them to undertake all their tasks on
equal terms with men. The pioneers of this great
reform, Mrs. William Grey and Miss Shirreff; Miss
Buss, the founder and head of the North London School;
the head of Cheltenham College; the founders of Girton
and Newnham, of Somerville Hall, and Lady Margaret's
Hall, have not only helped hundreds of young minds
to all the joys of high intellectual pursuits and lifted
them out of the dreary round of the old showy and
frivolous "accomplishments" wherein the youth of my
contemporaries was tormented, but they have prepared
the way,—the only safe and sound way—for all the
future achievements of our sex in the fields of
literature and public work.

By their aid at last the education of women has been
pushed so far that it became impossible longer to
refuse to recognize its success by University Degrees;
and henceforth women may stand not only *actually* (as
they have sometimes done before) but *admittedly* on a
level, as regards knowledge, with men.

Having gained so great a vantage ground on our
upward way, it can, I think, only depend on women
themselves, how far their entrance into public and
political life shall proceed. One thing only can stop
us, and that is the appearance of such disorders and
scandals, the betrayal of such a lack of good sense
amongst us, as shall make men (and the wiser women

also !) cry "Hold ! Let us go no farther !" The opinions of men, Eastern and Western alike, has hitherto been that unless women were restrained, kept in the narrowest grooves of custom and authority, they would infallibly run into outrageous folly and vice: and the example unhappily, of some ages of comparative emancipation (notably that of the Roman Empire) has tended to corroborate this view. Women used the liberty they then acquired as a cloak, —or rather as as facility, without any cloak at all,— for licentiousness.

Be it our part, my friends ! I implore you to aid with all our power of example and voice to show that Liberty *now*, for the women of England shall have a different result, and that, as it has been the nurse of noblest Virtue for men, so it shall be the nurse of purest virtue for us. And let us, as the needful beginning of such a true liberation, take uttermost precaution, that we adopt no habits, assume no freedoms which, even if they might be safe for ourselves individually, might be unsafe for other women. Better to forego for a time some of the privileges which our sex shall hereafter enjoy, than imperil by any laxity, any want of caution and wisdom now, the whole character of this great reformation.

We now turn directly to consider how stands the Duty of Women in England as regards entrance into public life and development of public spirit. What ought we to do at present, as concerns all public work wherein it is possible for us to obtain a share ?

The question seems to answer itself in its mere statement. We are bound to do *all* we can to promote the virtue and happiness of our fellow men and women, and *therefore* we must accept and seize every instrument of power, every vote, every influence which we can obtain to enable us to promote virtue and happiness. To return to the thought which to me seems so beautiful and fertile,—we must, if we desire to spread the "Kingdom of God," necessarily desire and seek the *means* by which we can extend it far and wide through the whole world. I am unable to imagine such a paradoxical person as one who should earnestly wish that Justice and Truth and Love should prevail, and yet should decline to accept the direct and natural means of influencing the affairs of his country in the direction of Justice, Truth, and Love.

All true Enthusiasm of Humanity, all genuine love of Justice, it seems to me, must spur those who feel it, to do what in them lies, not merely to exert the small powers they may find in their hands, but also to strive to obtain *more extended* powers of beneficence.

When one of us, women, sees a wrong needing to be righted, or a good to be achieved, or a truth to be taught, or a misery to be relieved, we wish for wealth, for influence, for the tongue of an orator, or the pen of a poet to achieve our object. These are

holy wishes, sacred longings of our heart, which come
to us in life's best hours and in the presence of God.
And why are not we also to wish and strive to be
allowed to place our hands on that vast machinery
whereby, in a constitutional realm, the great work of
the world is carried on, and which achieves by its enormous power tenfold either the good or the harm which
any individual can reach ; which may be turned to good
or turned to harm, according to the hands which touch
it ? In almost every case it is only by legislation (as you
all know) that the *roots* of great evils can be touched at
all, and that the social diseases of pauperism and vice
and crime can be brought within hope of cure. Women,
with the tenderest hearts and best intentions, go on
labouring all their life-times often in merely pruning the
offshoots of these evil roots,—in striving to allay and
abate the symptoms of the disease. But the nobler
and much more truly philanthropic work of plucking
up the roots, or curing the disease, they have been
forced to leave to men.

You will judge from these remarks the ground on
which, as a matter of *Duty,* I place the demand for
woman's political emancipation.   I think we are bound
to seek it in the first place, as a *means,* a very great
means, *of doing good,* fulfilling our Social Duty of
contributing to the virtue and happiness of mankind ;
advancing the kingdom of God. There are many
other reasons, viewed from the point of expediency ;
but this is the view from that of Duty. We know

too well that men who possess political rights do not always, or often, regard them in this fashion; but this is no reason why we should not do so. We also know that the individual power of one vote at any election seems rarely to effect any appreciable difference; but this also need not trouble us, for, little or great, if we can obtain any influence at all, we ought to seek for it; and the multiplication of the votes of women bent on securing conscientious candidates would soon make them not only appreciable, but weighty. Nay, further, the *direct* influence of a vote is but a small part of the power which the possession of the political franchise confers; its indirect influence is far more important. In a government like ours where the basis of representation is so immensely extensive, the whole business of legislation is carried on *by pressure*—the pressure of each represented class and party to get its grievances redressed, to make its interests prevail. The non-represented classes necessarily go to the wall, not by mere wilful neglect on the part of either ministers or members of Parliament, but because they must attend to their constituents first and to their pressure (they would lose their places and seats if they did not)—and the time for attending to the non-represented people, amid the hurry and bustle of the Session, never arrives. To be *one of a represented class* is a very much greater thing in England than merely to drop a paper into a ballot-box. It means to be able to *insist* upon attention to the wants of that class; and to all other matters of public importance which may be deemed deserving of attention. It is one of the sore grievances of women in particular that, not possessing representation, the measures which concern them are for ever postponed to the bills promoted by the represented classes (*e.g.*, the Married Woman's Property Bill was, if I mistake not, six times set down for reading in one Session in vain, the House being counted out on every occasion).

Thus in asking for the Parliamentary franchise we are asking, as I understand it, for the power to influence legislature generally ; and in every other kind of franchise, municipal, parochial, or otherwise, for similar power to bring our sense of justice and righteousness to bear on Public affairs. To achieve so great an end we ought all to be willing to incur trouble, and labour, and the loss of that privacy we some of us so highly value; with the ridicule and obloquy of silly men and sillier women.

What is this, after all, my friends, but *Public Spirit* —in one shape called Patriotism, in another, Philanthropy—the extension of our sympathies beyond the narrow bounds of our homes ; the disinterested enthusiasm for every good and sacred cause ? As I said at first, all the world has recognized from the earliest times, how good and noble and wholesome a thing it is for *men* to have their breasts filled with such Public Spirit; and we look upon them when they exhibit it as glorified thereby. Do you think it is not just as ennobling a thing for a *woman's* soul to be likewise filled with these large and generous and unselfish

emotions ? Do you think *she* does not rise, even as
man does, by stretching beyond the petty interests of
personal vanity or family ambition, and feeling her
heart throb with pride for the glory of her country,
with indignation against wrongs and injustices and per-
fidies and with the ardent longing to bring about some
great step of progress, some sorely needed reform ?

Nay, my friends, so infinitely valuable and ennobling
does it seem to me for women to partake of these
public interests, that, were it only for the moral
elevation of women themselves, I should desire them
to do so. The necessarily narrow and personal way
of thinking of all subjects ; the inveterate and stupid
habit of forming judgments, not on large and general
principles, but on one or two chance examples known
to themselves, and bringing in what Mr. A. or Mrs. B.
did, or this person or the other said, whenever such
subjects are under debate ; the small rivalries for
small social distinctions ; the hollow friendships founded
on mere idle companionships ; the miserable, endless
domestic squabbles filling up time and thoughts ; all
these and many another deplorable weakness of our
sex, seem to me curable only by the influx of fresh
and noble interests ; interests neither concerning our
own aggrandizement, nor that of our husbands and
children. For petty thoughts and small aims, here
are large ones ; for trivial companionships, here are
almost sacred friendships founded on the community
of noble and disinterested aims.

I have often thought how strange it is that men can at one and the same moment, cheerfully consign our sex to lives either of narrowest toil, or senseless luxury and vanity ; and then sneer at the smallness of our aims, the pettiness of our thoughts, the puerility of our conversation ! Are we, then, made of different stuff, that the *régime* which would make Hercules pusillanimous and effeminate, should make us courageous and noble-minded ?

But there is a special reason why we, women of the upper classes in England, should at this time stir ourselves to obtain influence in public affairs. That reason is, the miserable oppressions, the bitter griefs, the cruel wrongs our sister women are doomed to suffer, and which might be relieved and righted by better legislation. I have explained just now how every unrepresented class in a constitutional country *must* be neglected by ministers and members of Parliament,—and in the case of women there are such enormous arrears of bad laws regarding them lying over from far off times of barbarism and needing now to be revised, that this difficulty of obtaining attention to our concerns is a double cruelty. Instead of needing no legislation, because their interests are so well cared for (as some senators have audaciously asserted)—I boldly affirm that there is no class of men in England who could not better, and with less consequent injustice, forego the franchise, than women.

There are thousands of poor women who suffer

the worst of these wrongs; some who are placed
legally at the mercy of savage husbands, or who are
driven by misery and ill-paid, hopeless labour into
the Dead Sea of vice; and some, of a little higher class
whose children are torn from their arms, perhaps to
satisfy a dead or a living husband's religious fanati-
cism. These most piteously wronged of all God's
creatures, are breaking their hearts day by day and
year by year all around us; no *man* much understand-
ing their woes; no *man* having leisure to seek their
remedy. And can *we* sit patiently by, and know all
these things, and long to relieve all this agony and
stop all these wrongs, and yet accept contentedly as
a beautiful dispensation—not of God but of man,—
the law which leaves us tongue-tied and hand-
bound, unable to throw the weight of one poor vote
into the scale of justice and mercy? Can we think
our wretched drawing-room dignities and courtesies,
and the smiles and approval of a swarm of fops and
fools worth preserving at the cost of the knowledge
that we *might* do something to lift up this load, and
do it *not*?

Needless, I hope, it is to add that we must come to
these public duties,—whenever we may be permitted
to fulfil them,—in the most conscientious and disinterested spirit, and determined to perform them
excellently well. Approaching them from the side I
have indicated, this can scarcely fail to be the case;
and we must all bear in mind that for a long time to

come every step women take in the field of politics
will be watched by not-unnaturally prejudiced spec-
tators of the innovation; and that to show either
indifference towards the acquirement of new powers,
or misuse or neglect of those we already possess,
cannot fail to be recorded in damning characters
against our whole movement.

Practically, I think that every woman who has any
margin of time or money to spare should adopt some
one public interest, some philanthropic undertaking,
or some social agitation of reform, and give to that
cause whatever time and work she may be able to
afford; thus completing her life by adding to her
private duties the noble effort to advance God's
Kingdom beyond the bounds of her home. Remember,
pray,—that I say emphatically " *adding* to her private
duties,"—not *subtracting* from them. I should think
it a most grievous and deplorable error to neglect any
private duties already incurred for the sake of new
public duties subsequently adopted. But in truth
though we read of "Mrs. Jellybys'" in novels, I have
failed yet to find, in a pretty large experience of real life,
a single case in which a woman who exercised Public
Spirit, even to the extent of self-devotion, was not *also*
an admirable and conscientious daughter, wife, mother,
or mistress of a household. This spectre of the
Female Politician who abandons her family to neglect,
for the sake of passing bills in Parliament, is just as
complete an illusion of the masculine brain as the

older spectre whom Sydney Smith laid by a joke; the woman who would "forsake an infant for a quadratic equation."

One point, however, I ought to touch upon here. The question is, *Who* are the women who should consider themselves free to devote any considerable time to what we may call Out-Door work—Philanthropic or Political? Daughters living with their parents in easy circumstances? Wives? or Mothers? My own view, (founded on the principles on which we have proceeded all along) is this—

I think nearly all women of the educated classes might afford at least so much time to politics as to be able to form an intelligent opinion and give an intelligent *vote*, in every constituency, Parochial or Educational, Municipal or Parliamentary, to which they may be admitted. Men who perform the most arduous professions find time to do this; and there seems no adequate reason why the busiest housewives or daughters should not do the same. At all events, there need never be more women than there now are men, who neglect to use their political rights.

Then, I think, that the great majority of grown-up unmarried women, living in their parent's homes, would surely find time at least to begin some philanthropic work, and *train on* to public usefulness, if it were (as it ought to be) assumed in their families that it was natural and proper for them so to do. There would always remain a considerable proportion of young

women whose whole energies must be devoted to the
sacred cares of aged or blind or invalid parents, or of
one parent alone when the other is dead ; and there
are, perhaps, straitened means to be eked out, or infant
brothers and sisters to be tended and taught.   But
outside of these, there are (as we all know) hundreds of
ladies between the ages of twenty and forty or fifty,
whose whole filial duties do not occupy an hour or
two a day.   The parents of daughters of this class are
now, at last, generally awakening to the duty of allowing
and encouraging them to find such work as they may
well and safely perform (not always an easy selection !),
and this awakening I trust will go on till the whole
stupid notion of " genteel idleness " be swept from the
world.   But Rome was not built in a day, and we must
have patience to see this reformation carried out by
degrees.   Among parents of only moderate fortune who
cannot leave their daughters in thorough comfort and
freedom as regards money, I confess I think the first
thing to be done is to give them such special training
as may be needed to put them in the way of earning
money for themselves.   When this is needless, it ought
to be no less imperative duty to help them to use the
wealth they will inherit, and the leisure at their disposal,
in some gratuitous labour of love for the poor, the sick,
the ignorant, the blind ; for animals ; in short, in
any cause of humanity ; but above all in the cause of
their own sex, and the relief of the misery of their
sisters.

When it comes to the question of Married women
during the years wherein they frequently become
mothers, devoting themselves to any considerable
extent, either to earning money for their families, or
performing gratuitous out-door public service,—I
must say my opinion is different. So *immense* are
the claims on a Mother, physical claims on her bodily
and brain vigour, and moral claims on her heart and
thoughts, that she cannot, I believe, meet them all,
and find any large margin beyond for other cares and
work. She serves the community in the very best
and highest way it is possible to do, by giving birth
to healthy children, whose physical strength has not
been defrauded, and to whose moral and mental nurture
she can give the whole of her thoughts. This is her
Function, Public and Private, at once,—the *Profession* which she has adopted. No higher can be
found; and in my judgment it is a misfortune to all
concerned when a woman, under such circumstances,
is either driven by poverty or lured by any generous
ambition, to add to that great "Profession of a
Matron," any other systematic work; either as
bread-winner to the family, or as a philanthropist
or politician. Of course all this ceases when a
woman's family is complete and her children are grown
up and no longer need her devotion. She may then
enter, or return to public life with the immeasurable
gain of rich experience of a Mother's heart. But as
I have said, till her children no longer need her, I

11

look upon it as a mistake and a calamity if a Mother undertake any other great work to interfere with the one which would be enough to absorb the largest and noblest woman's nature ever created.

It is time that these Addresses should now conclude. You have done me much honour in coming to hear me, and much favour in hearing me so patiently. I thank you heartily for your kindness : you, my old friends, whose dear faces smile on me on every side ; and you who were before unknown to me, but between whom and myself there will be henceforth, I hope, always some bond of sympathy, even if I have failed to carry you with me in every step of this long journey which we have now made together. Our hearts must, surely, have touched at many points, and we have at least been conscious of meeting for a good intent; that of studying our common duties. I have felt it to be very presumptuous on my part (probably fulfilling those duties less well than half of you; certainly less well than many I know), to offer thus to address you; but, I fear, if I waited till I had better learned my own lesson, the years of vigour to speak at all (now so quickly passing from me) would all have run. The night cometh when no man can work. I spent many a day and many a long night studying the science of ethics, and learning what the greatest minds of all ages have thought about it, years before many of you, here present, were born,—

and in years when you, who are my contemporaries, were perhaps more naturally engaged in dancing and playing, and thinking of love and marriage! If I have succeeded in leading you to think a little more *distinctly* than you have hitherto done on this great subject, and induced you to bring your more or less vague impressions into shape, and to test them by the larger principles of morality, I shall have done something, since an opinion otherwise formed is not, in truth, a *judgment,* but only a *prejudice,* a pre-judgment.

But it is not only to *think* out the problems of Duty—but surely also to *act* upon your conclusions, whereto all these poor exhortations of mine should lead you, had I the power of persuasion. I want to lure you to *lead a dutiful life,* not merely to *talk* and *think* soundly of duty. None of us, I am sure, realize how blessed a thing we might make of our lives if we would but do this, if we would but give ourselves, heart and soul, to fulfil *all* the obligations Personal, Social and Religious which rest upon us ;—to gain the strength,—

> To think, to feel, to do
> Only the holy Right.
> To yield no step in the awful race,
> No blow in the fearful fight;

—to live in purity and truth and courage, a life of love to God and to man, striving to make every spot where we dwell, every region to which our influence can extend, *God's Kingdom,* where his will shall be done on earth as it is done in heaven.

We are, many of us, in these days wandering far
and wide in despairing search for some bread of life
whereby we may sustain our souls, some *Holy Grail*
wherein we may drink salvation from doubt and sin.
It may be a long, long quest ere we find it; but one
thing is ready to our hands. It is DUTY! Let us turn
to that, in simple fidelity, and labour to act up to our
own highest ideal, to *be* the very best and purest and
truest we know how, and to *do* around us every work
of love which our hands and hearts may reach. When
we have lived and laboured like this, then, I believe,
that the light will come to us, as to many another
doubting soul, and it will prove true once more that
"they who do God's will shall know of his doctrine;"
and they who strive to advance his kingdom here
will gain faith in another Divine realm beyond the
dark River, where Virtue shall ascend into Holiness,
and Duty be transfigured into Joy.

THE END.

G. NORMAN AND SON, PRINTERS, 29, MAIDEN LANE, COVENT GARDEN.

For EU product safety concerns, contact us at Calle de José Abascal, 56–1°,
28003 Madrid, Spain or eugpsr@cambridge.org.